Judy Richter's
RIDING for KIDS

Judy Richter's
RIDING for KIDS

The mission of Storey Publishing is to serve our customers by publishing practical information that encourages personal independence in harmony with the environment.

Edited by Deborah Burns
Art direction and editorial assistance by Meredith Maker
Cover design by Wendy Palitz and Laurie Baker
Cover photographs: Top left, lower right © James Leslie Parker/Benson Photography; top right, lower left © Shelley Heatley
Text design and production by Eugenie S. Delaney
Production assistance by Kelley Nesbit
Illustrations by JoAnna Rissanen
Diagrams by Chuck Galey
All photography by Shelley Heatley, except for the following: Judy Richter: v, x, xi bottom, xii, 73, 84, 85, 87 top, 107, 108, 110; © Benson Photography: 35, 94; © Cansports: 97; © Equestrian Photographic Services: 62; © Kym Ketcham: 57; © Richard Killian: 56 top; © 2002 Photography by O'Neill's: 63, 80; © James Leslie Parker/Benson Photography: 88; © Phelpsphotos.com: 53 bottom; Giles Prett: ix, 19, 109; © Tobé Saskor: 53 top and middle; ©Lesley Ward: 104, 105, 111

Special thanks to Dianna Robin Dennis
Indexed by Susan Olason/Indexes and Knowledge Maps
Glossary compiled by Lisa H. Hiley

Printed in Hong Kong by Elegance Printing
10 9 8 7 6 5 4 3 2 1

Library of Congress Cataloging-in-Publication Data

Richter, Judy.

Riding for kids / Judy Richter.

p. cm.

Summary: Provides abundant photographs and detailed information describing how to ride a horse, from dress and equipment to jumping and competition.

ISBN 1-58017-511-2 (alk. paper) — ISBN 1-58017-510-4 (pbk. : alk. paper)

1.   Horsemanship—Juvenile literature. [1. Horsemanship.] I. Title.

SF309.2.R52 2003
798.2—dc21   203045842

Dedication

To my granddaughters, Maxine and Margot Richter, who are just starting to learn to ride, and to my parents, Philip B. and Mary K. Hofmann, who met on horseback many years ago and founded a family of riders.

Acknowledgments

This book could not have happened without the encouragement and assistance of many.

Mentors: George Morris, Bill Steinkraus, Bert de Nemethy, to name a few

Storey Publishing: Meredith Maker and Deborah Burns

Photographer: Shelley Heatley

Riders: Brianne and Clementine Goutal, Haley and Lindsay Heatley, Schaefer Raposa, Annie Starke, and many others

Instructors: Peter Lutz and Mary Manfredi

Madelyn Larsen, literary agent extraordinaire, for her encouragement over the years

Kathy Farina, typist and helper, who gets things done quickly

My family — husband Max and sons, Hans (and wife, Jennifer) and Philip — for their staunch support always

Last, but not least, the many horses and ponies that have taught me so much and enriched my life

Contents

A Note to Parents

THIS BOOK IS INTENDED FOR YOUNG PEOPLE who are just starting their riding careers. With very young children, it is sufficient to have a carefully supervised leadline ride on a quiet pony or to sit in front of an adult on a quiet horse. If properly done, that will spark children's interest, and they will feel comfortable around horses and ponies. Remember that to a little child, even the smallest pony looks gigantic.

Zealous parents often want their children to start riding too young. I prefer to start riding lessons at about age seven, when the child has gained sufficient strength not to topple off if the pony sneezes. Also by age seven, children have started school; most are ready to take instruction and are able to learn to ride.

Once a child has turned seven, has the coordination to ride, and is eager for lessons, then a parent has to search around for the best place to start. If you are a parent who does not ride or know much about horses, consult the Yellow Pages and visit some local stables. Word of mouth can give you good leads. The best source

Seven is about the right age to begin riding lessons.

Riding rings, whether indoor or outdoor, should be orderly and tidy.

Look for a neat, clean, workmanlike establishment. Glitz and glamor may mask considerable mediocrity. Remember, you want your child to become a horseman, not just a rider.

of information, however, is the United States Equestrian Federation (USEF), a national organization of horse shows and related activities. No matter where you live, the USEF will know at least one good riding establishment near you.

Before you sign up your child, go and see the place, meet the instructor or instructors, watch some lessons, and speak to other parents there. Most important, you must feel it is a safe place. If you observe situations that seem dangerous to you — youngsters on horses that seem too fresh, horses out of control, casual instructors — look elsewhere.

In a well-organized tack room, everything has a place: the bridles, saddles, pads, crops, and spurs.

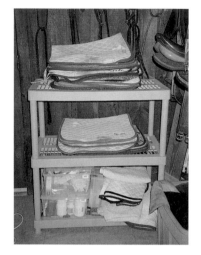

Shelves make a great place to store saddle pads and leg wraps.

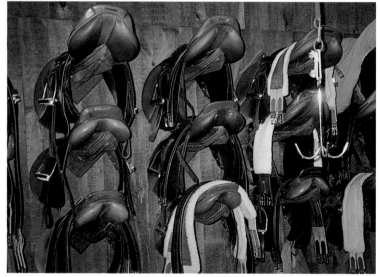

Crops and spurs find a home in old wastebaskets and woven baskets.

The stable itself should be neat and clean. "Glitz" has become very fashionable in recent years, but it is not at all important. Furthermore, it is expensive. A fancy place often masks considerable mediocrity. Several rings full of all the latest jumps and a barn full of brass and chrome can fool someone who doesn't look beyond the surface. A workmanlike barn will serve your purposes much better, for you want your child to be a horseman, not just a rider.

The facilities will tell you a lot about the instructor. Even a parent who knows nothing about horses can tell if the horses are well cared for. Are they clean and well fed? Are the stalls and yard neat and clean? If the instructor is a poor caretaker and a slob, his or her teaching will also be mediocre and sloppy. Horses and riders alike will not ever "be all they can be" in such an environment. If you have a bad feeling about the place, trust your instincts and look elsewhere.

Recently I judged a horse show and gave a clinic in Alaska. To my surprise, there were numerous good riding establishments in that state. With the Internet and the proliferation of satellite dishes, people there can be as current as anyone else on what is happening throughout the horse world. Even in remote areas, you can find a quality school.

This light, airy Florida stable has ceiling fans to increase the flow of air through the many open doors and windows. Notice how clean and tidy this facility is.

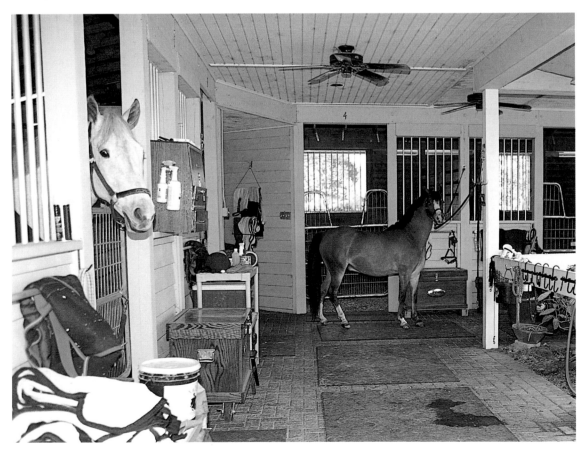

Observe the instructor's style and attitude. Annie's instructor, Mary Manfredi, is giving her a jumping lesson here. Annie is just a bit ahead of her horse because she needs to have more weight in her heels. Positive correction of a minor fault is what works; shouting achieves nothing.

Speak briefly with the instructor. Make it a habit from the start not to monopolize his or her time. The focus should be on your child's interest, ability, and goals. Likewise, encourage your child to "fit in" and accept the discipline of the trainer. You will sense right away if this is the kind of person you want your child to associate with and be influenced by. Remember that your child will absorb a lot more at the stable than simply learning to ride a horse. The instructor is responsible first for your child's safety and ultimately for his or her progress as a rider and as a person.

Be realistic about finances. Riding and showing horses can be a very expensive sport. If the instructor has some notion of your financial commitment, he will be able to guide you so you can do as much as possible for your child but remain within your means. You will do your child no favors if you overextend your finances and then lay a guilt trip on him or her for your extravagance!

Riding is a sport in which women may and do compete with men on an equal basis, even at the Olympic level. At the novice levels, girls sometimes catch on more quickly than boys, probably because they are not quite as distracted by other sports such as soccer, hockey, and football. By the time children are competing at horse shows, the girls usually outnumber the boys and often win those early competitions. At this age we do lose a lot of boy riders — the fragile ones who hate being beaten by girls — but the tough, talented ones who truly love it and stick with it end up as very good riders.

Riding is certainly no "girls' sport" at any level, so encourage boys not to give it up for that reason. Be sure there are other men and boys riding at the place you select for your son. He needs good role models, or he will soon lose interest and join his friends on the soccer or football field.

Children with learning disabilities benefit tremendously from learning how to ride. A kindly horse soon becomes a wonderful and patient friend. The discipline of the lessons, learning diagonals at the trot and leads at the canter, helps them manage difficulties with handedness and coordination. Just simple exercises like making sure their hard hats and boots are in the car ready for the lesson help them learn to plan and organize their lives. I know many learning-disabled children who have become excellent riders. If your child has a learning disability, be sure to let the instructor know, so he or she can make appropriate adjustments to your child's program. Most trainers have pupils with learning disabilities and are well able to help them become good riders.

For physically and emotionally handicapped children, horseback riding can be an excellent sport and great therapy as well. For information about riding programs for the handicapped in your area, see the appendix.

> Your child will absorb a lot more at the stable than simply learning to ride a horse. The instructor is responsible first for your child's safety and ultimately for his or her progress as a rider and as a person.

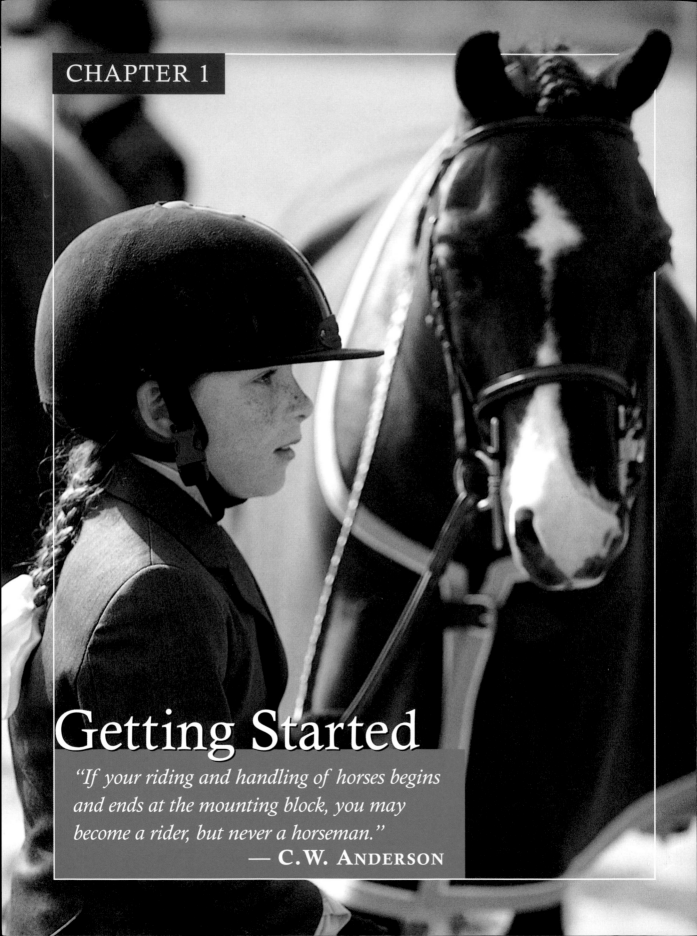

CHAPTER 1

Getting Started

"If your riding and handling of horses begins and ends at the mounting block, you may become a rider, but never a horseman."
— C.W. ANDERSON

L EARNING TO RIDE is not easy, but it is lots of fun. What makes riding more fun than any other sport is that you are involved with a pony or a horse. Every **equine** has his own personality, quirks, and certain things that he does better than others. The best riders are those who understand their mounts. Cruelty or abuse does not persuade them, nor does spoiling. Ponies and horses do best when they understand their job. The good ones want to do it right; the spoiled ones and those with a bad character do not. Most ponies and horses have good characters. Some, of course, are more generous than others.

Horse Talk

chaps:
Leather pants with no seat, worn to protect a rider's legs.

equine:
The family of animals including horses, ponies, and . . . zebras!

jodhpurs:
Snug-fitting riding pants.

Proper and Safe Dress

Once you and your family have decided where you will take riding lessons, you will need to make sure you have suitable clothes and equipment. The correct attire for riding includes a regulation hard hat/helmet (approved by the USEF) that fits properly, with its chin strap snugly adjusted. **Never ride without one.** Girls should develop early the habit of putting their hair up and wearing a hairnet. (See page 81.)

The second must for riding is a pair of shoes or boots with heels. Sneakers and other flat shoes can slide through the stirrups, and a rider could be dragged to death by a frightened pony. (In my barn, riders who "forget" their boots have to ride without stirrups that day. The good news is that these riders will develop a good tight leg whether or not they want to.)

A USEF-approved helmet is a must for all types of riding, but any shirt and jeans will do for a start.

The right foul-weather gear will keep you comfortable and help protect your clothes and boots.

Attire should always be neat and clean, with the shirt tucked into correctly fitting jeans or **jodhpur** pants. Jeans are appropriate at most stables for basic lessons and pleasure riding. Riders who are very keen and ride often can buy leather **chaps** to use every day to prevent their legs from becoming chafed. The chaps, whether ready-made or custom made, are available at most saddlery shops. Look in the Yellow Pages of your telephone directory for the name of a tack shop or saddlery store near where you live, so you are safely and correctly dressed.

Foul-Weather Gear

Here are some hints for cold-weather riding.

- Sheepskin-lined boots are warm, but remember that they must have heels and must be able to move freely in your stirrup irons. If they are too wide, you risk catching a foot in the iron, which can be dangerous.
- At winter horse shows, wear a pair of rubbers with sheepskin or heavy felt innersoles over your regular riding boots for extra warmth. They can be removed just before you enter the ring.
- When taking a lesson in cold weather, don't wear a huge, puffy, goose-down parka that will prevent your instructor from seeing your upper body. Wear a vest or windbreaker under the parka, so you can shed layers when you have warmed up.
- Veteran horse show riders always bring a warm parka, good rain gear, and rubbers to every horse show — even on the warmest, sunniest day. Benefit from their experience and develop the habit early, so you won't get frozen or soaked.
- Even the early-morning dew on the grass can be hard on your boots. Rubbers save a lot of wear and tear on your boots, so always keep them handy.

Getting Dressed

Before saddling and bridling your pony, you must get dressed for riding. First the hard hat must be snapped in place. The chin strap should be snug. Harness hats are required by the United States Equestrian Federation (USEF) for all riders under 18 while competing at their recognized horse shows. This is a good rule for children and adults alike.

1. Haley snaps her helmet on. The chin strap should be snug. It is a good idea to wear your helmet even when working around your horse in the barn.

2. The spurs are buckled to the outside with the straps pointing down. If a strap is long, cut it off or tuck it under the spur, so it does not flap against the boot.

(Continued on next page)

3. Next are the chaps, which are very handy for everyday wear. Made of leather, they can be ready-made or custom made. They fit neatly over jeans and offer good protection to the legs. Riding in jeans can cause sores on the knees and legs. (Jodhpurs and boots are always correct also.) The chaps buckle in front and zippers go down the legs on the outside.

4. Now Haley is fully dressed, so she carries her saddle and bridle from the tack room to where her pony is cross-tied.

Some horses need spurs; others do not. Weather conditions are often a factor. Spurs are usually needed more in warm weather than in cold. Few horses need spurs in big open fields. Many need them in small and/or spooky rings. **Use spurs only under your trainer's supervision.** Beginners should not use spurs until they have established a strong, steady lower leg. Loose legs armed with spurs can cause a horse to run away.

For riders who do all their own grooming and stable work, chaps are handy because they can be put on and taken off quickly and easily.

Grooming Your Pony

Before every ride, your pony should be groomed. Removing the dirt from his coat will help to eliminate itchy skin and saddle soreness and keep him looking and feeling his best. Most ponies love to be fussed over, so don't rush. Grooming is a good chance to bond with your pony and also to thoroughly check him over for any cuts or bruises he may have gotten in the pasture or stall.

Here is the proper way to lead a pony. Lindsay is on his left side. With her right hand, she holds the rope close to his chin and with her left holds the end of the rope so it does not trail on the ground. **Never wrap the rope around your hand or arm.**

Lindsay is cross-tying her pony to groom him and tack him up. Always put the saddle on first, unhook the cross ties, and then put the bridle on. Never cross-tie a horse by the bridle, for he could become startled and tear up the bridle as well as his mouth.

Here is the equipment needed for grooming and riding:
A. boot polish and brushes, **B.** rub rag, **C.** scraper, **D.** sponge, **E.** hoof dressing, **F.** saddle soap and sponge, **G.** dandy brush (stiff bristles) and body brush (soft bristles), **H.** scrub mitt, **I.** hole punch, **J.** crop, **K.** spurs, **L.** gloves, **M.** curry comb, **N.** mane comb, **O.** hoof pick.

Grooming Tools

How to use the equipment for grooming:

1. Use the curry comb with a circular motion to loosen dirt and hair.

2. Use the dandy brush (stiff bristles) first, then follow with the body brush (soft bristles). Brush the hair in the direction it grows. Brush tail hair gently so as not to pull it all out!

3. Smooth down the hair with the rub rag (a great use for old towels!).

4. Use the hoof pick to pick out your horse's feet before and after riding. Use the brush end to remove mud caked on the outside of his feet.

5. Apply hoof dressing before riding to dress him up and after to keep his hooves from drying out.

Use a soft brush, not a stiff dandy brush, on your horse's face. Some horses prefer the softer brush for their entire body. A horse will let you know by flinching if his skin is too sensitive for the harder brush.

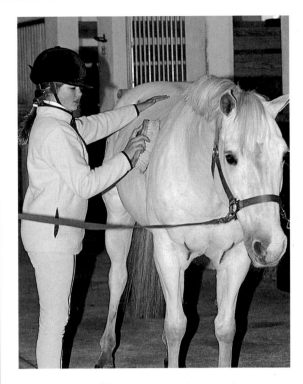

Haley curried her pony with round sweeping strokes to loosen the dirt and hair. Now she is brushing him all over, head to tail, under his belly and down his legs, being careful to brush in the same direction that his hair grows.

Using the hoof pick, she picks the dirt out of his feet. To pick out his left feet, front and hind, she faces the rear and runs her left hand down his leg to the pastern, the area just below his ankle and above his hoof. Sometimes she has to lean on his shoulder to displace his weight to the other foot.

Tacking Up Your Pony

Many stables have the ponies all "tacked up" — saddled and bridled for their riders — when they come for lessons. Make it your business to find out how to saddle and bridle the pony properly. Watch others tack up their horses and ask your instructor to show you how to do it.

Of course, you want to be able to do it correctly, for it is a big responsibility indeed. The Resources section lists some books that clearly explain all the details of stable management.

The Saddle

Stables that offer beginner riding lessons provide the saddle. A child who rides often will eventually need her own. Your trainer and local tack or saddlery shop are very helpful in selecting a saddle that fits properly.

Always put on the saddle before the bridle, so the pony remains cross-tied and does not wander around the aisle and step on your toes as you saddle him.

1. Haley places the pad on her pony's back for protection. Then she sets her saddle gently on top of it.

2. Next she tightens the girth. Not too tight yet — she does that just before she mounts.

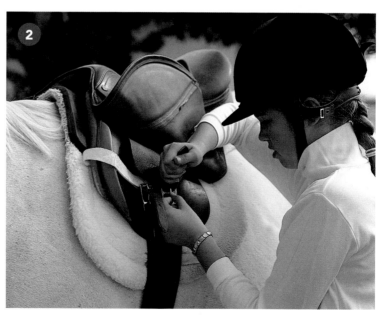

Once mounted, the rider should always check the girth before starting the day's work. Most ponies and horses tend to "blow up" — that is, puff out their bellies by holding their breath in an effort to prevent the girth from being pulled tight.

3. Here the saddle is in place with the stirrup irons pulled up and the stirrup leathers tucked in properly. Never leave the stirrups down; they can catch on something as the horse walks by, or simply bang against his sides and startle him.

Now is a good time to check that the stirrups are the right length for you. They should be as long as the length of your arm. Always remember to run the stirrups back up and tuck the leathers through.

Like people, ponies have their quirks. Some of the kindest and most well-behaved mounts have "cold backs" or are cinchy. If cinched up too suddenly, they react by bucking and thrashing. This particular quirk is easy to deal with, but if it's overlooked, a serious accident can result. Therefore, never make the girth very tight at first.

1. First, Haley slips the bit into her pony's mouth, being careful not to put her fingers between his teeth. (Press his lip gently against his teeth to open his mouth if he resists.) Next, she puts his bridle on gently over his ears, first left and then right.

The Bridle

Be sure the saddle is on securely while the pony is still cross-tied. Then put on the bridle. First, put the reins over his head onto his neck so that he can't escape. Then grasp the cheekpieces with your right hand and use your left hand to open his mouth. Pull his top lip over a tooth if he does not open his mouth for you. Then gently poke his ears — first left and then right — through the crownpiece. Finally, buckle up the noseband and the throatlatch. Allow four fingers' worth of space between his throat and the strap.

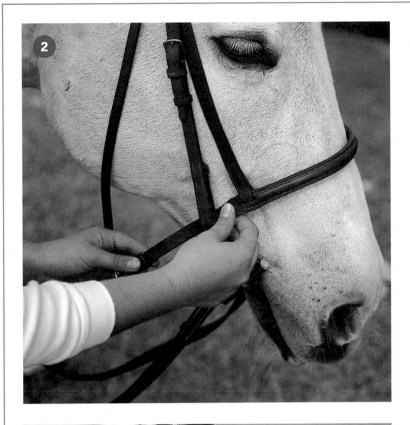

2. Now the noseband is tucked under the cheek-piece and buckled shut. Notice that it is just under the protruding bone on the side of his head.

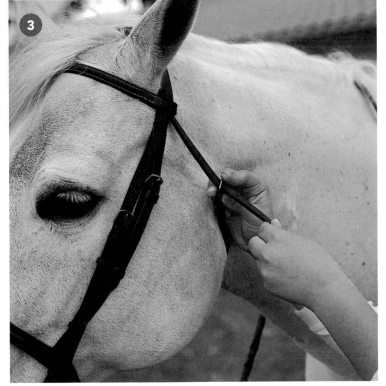

3. To finish, Haley buckles the throatlatch shut: not too tight to choke him, not so loose that it slaps up and down. You should be able just to slip your hand between the throatlatch and his throat.

Mounting

Take the reins over the pony's head and lead him from the barn to where you plan to mount. Make sure the saddle's girth is tight enough. Check your stirrup length against your arm's length, as shown on page 9. Gather the reins in your left hand. Stand by his shoulder, facing the rear of the pony, and insert your left foot in the stirrup with your toe against the girth (not his ribs). Grasp the back of the saddle and hoist yourself up.

Here Haley uses a lengthened stirrup to make mounting easier. She gathers her reins, then puts her toe in the stirrup, pressing toward the girth so as not to jab her pony in the stomach and cause him to walk (or gallop) away. Once mounted, she will readjust her stirrup length.

Haley's pony is a little tall, so here she wisely seeks the mounting block. She stands at his shoulder and faces his hindquarters, so she can swing up quickly should he move off. Her reins should be short enough to prevent the pony's moving off when she is halfway up, but not too short, which might cause him to turn backward. Here, they are a little long.

Be careful not to land hard on the pony's back. Flopping on him may startle and even hurt him. Ponies and horses hate it when riders flop on their backs. It startles them and it hurts! There is no worse way to start your ride and your relationship with a pony.

If the pony is too tall to mount from the ground, use a mounting block or a fence rail. Another option is to lengthen your stirrup to make the ascent less difficult. A "leg up" from a friend is another good way to mount.

When there is no mounting block handy, a helpful friend can offer a leg up. Again, be careful to settle gently in the saddle.

A close-up of the proper way to hold the rider's leg for the "leg up." Some prefer to jump on the count of 1, others on 3. Learn to jump, so you are not like a sack of potatoes being heaved up onto the pony.

Get someone to hold your horse until you have mastered stirrup and girth adjustment.

Brianne has bridged her reins (gathered them in one hand), keeping them short for control, and her eyes are up. She keeps her foot in the stirrup while she presses the tongue of the buckle into the proper hole with her left index finger.

Stirrup Adjustment

Once mounted, double-check your stirrup length. With your feet out of your stirrups, the stirrup irons should hang at your anklebones. To shorten or lengthen a stirrup, take the reins in one hand and keep your foot in the stirrup as you adjust the length, as shown in the photograph below.

CORRECT

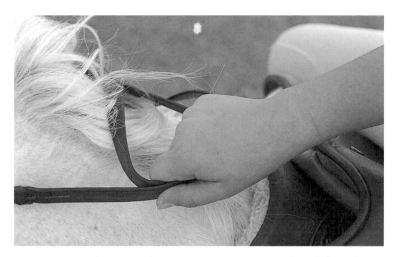

A close-up of bridged reins. When you need to have the reins in one hand, this is how to do it.

Here a friend is checking to make sure Haley's stirrups are "even," or of the same length.

INCORRECT

Having dropped her reins, Brianne has no control, which is a serious problem if her horse should bolt away. Her lowered eyes will not notice something that is approaching and could startle him. Here is an accident just waiting to happen!

CORRECT

Girth Adjustment

Once mounted, a rider should always check that the girth is tight enough. This is the rider's responsibility and no one else's. A loose girth can cause a life-threatening accident, for the saddle can slip off to the side or even under the horse's belly.

INCORRECT

Brianne's reins are bridged and she is looking ahead, not down.

CORRECT

Dangerous girth adjustment. Brianne has dropped her reins and is looking down, not at what is happening around her. She does not have any control should something startle her pony.

A close-up of Brianne's index finger pressing the tongue of the buckle into the hole. No need to look down; she can feel what she is doing.

Dismounting

In order to dismount properly, take the reins in your left hand, quietly remove both feet from your stirrups, and swing down. Always take the reins over the horse's head before you lead him into the barn.

1. Haley takes her feet out of the stirrups before swinging off.

2. She swings off, landing on both feet.

3. After dismounting, Haley slides each stirrup up the leather and tucks the strap through the stirrup iron.

The rider is always responsible for neat, clean turnout as well as proper tack adjustment.

Now Haley is leading her pony with the reins over his head and stirrups properly run up. Safety is a prime consideration here, as always. With the reins over his head, Haley has a lot more control should he scoot or shy. Stirrups banging on his sides could frighten him or get caught on something as they pass by. **The best way to prevent accidents is to make it a habit to do things properly in the first place.**

CORRECT

Putting the Horse Away

Part of being a team player is making sure your team-mate is put away properly. After you have finished your ride, make sure your pony is not soaked with sweat and blowing hard when you return to the stable. If he is hot and blowing, walk him in the ring or around the barn before you bring him inside. **Never put a horse away hot.** If you do, you are inviting all kinds of problems, the most likely one being laminitis, or founder.

Founder occurs when a horse's blood flows into his hoof faster than it flows out. The horse suffers terrible pain and, in a severe case, may even have to be put down . . . all because his rider was in too much of a hurry to cool him out properly.

Untacking

After your ride, lead your horse into the barn, locate his halter, remove the bridle, put on the halter, and cross-tie him. Then unbuckle the girth on both sides and put it across the saddle. Remove saddle, girth, and pads from his back. Put the saddle carefully on a saddle rack or lean it against the wall. Do not throw it on the floor and risk damaging the leather or the saddle tree.

If it is warm, sponge off the horse and walk him until he is dry and cool. Use warm water always — unless the weather is very hot. If soap is needed, be sure to rinse it all out. Usually two rinses are needed to get all the soap out. On cold days, simply rub him down with a towel, and when he is dry, brush him well. Before returning him to his stall, brush him and pick out his feet.

Don't forget to clean your tack! Rinse and dry the bit after every use. Clean your tack often and thoroughly. If your tack gets wet in the rain, dry it immediately with a towel before cleaning it.

After you have put your horse away, it's time to clean your tack. To clean the tack, you will need a pail of warm water, a couple of small sponges, and a bar of glycerin soap.

1. Dip a sponge into the water and wring it out.

2. Clean off the bit and then the bridle, martingale, saddle, and finally the girth, re-rinsing the sponge to get rid of the dirt.

3. Dampen the second sponge and rub it on the glycerin soap. Apply it to all the leather you are cleaning. Keep the soap off the bit — it tastes awful!

4. Once a month or so, polish the bit with metal polish (wash afterward to get rid of the taste) and treat the saddle and bridle with leather therapy oil.

Removing the Bridle

1. Haley prepares to untack her pony. Notice the halter on her shoulder, at hand so she can slip it on easily.

2. She slips off the bridle, but notice that the reins are still around his neck, just in case he decides to try to escape.

3. Now she puts on his halter. She removes the bridle first and cross-ties him before taking off the saddle.

Finishing Touches

1. Having recruited her sister, Lindsay, to hold their pony, Haley sponges his neck and back with warm water. On warm days when the pony is sweaty, a sponge bath is the best way to get him clean.

2. Next she scrapes off the excess water.

3. The pony is blanketed and ready for dinner and then bed. Although it was warm enough to bathe him, by evening it turned cool and he needed a lightweight blanket.

Rugging Up

At night your pony may need a sheet and one or more blankets, depending on the weather. Again, common sense tells you how to "rug him up," as the British say. Allow for temperature variations in stables, because some are much warmer than others. Also, the length and thickness of your pony's coat must be considered.

Here are some guidelines. Regardless of whether you live in Alaska or Florida, if you are wearing a sweater, he needs a sheet; a jacket, he needs a blanket; sweaters and a down jacket, he needs a sheet (next to the skin) and two blankets.

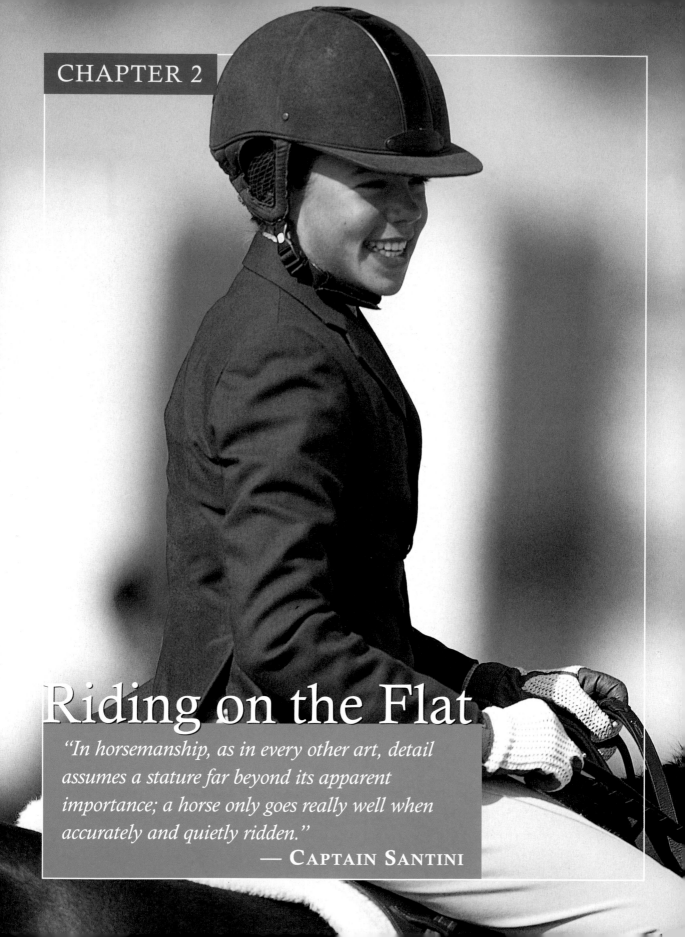

CHAPTER 2

Riding on the Flat

"In horsemanship, as in every other art, detail assumes a stature far beyond its apparent importance; a horse only goes really well when accurately and quietly ridden."

— **CAPTAIN SANTINI**

FROM THE VERY BEGINNING, it is important to concentrate on developing a good position. A good beginning will make all the difference later on. Develop good habits from the start and you will end up riding well. You'll have to check your position often until you become secure in the saddle.

The Rider's Position

The proper basic position at the halt is to have head, shoulder, hip, and heel all in line. Another imaginary line runs from the rider's elbow to the horse's mouth. Elbows should be just in front of the hips and hands should make an angle of about 45 degrees. Stirrup leathers should hang perpendicular to the ground. About two thirds of the rider's weight should be in the heels and one third on the saddle.

At the walk, trot, and canter the rider's body should be inclined a few degrees in front of the vertical. Your weight should always be in your heels. A good exercise even for beginners is to stand in the stirrups and force the weight into the heels. A rider with a deep heel does not get ahead of his horse — a major fault that creates countless problems later. So get in the habit of having a good, solid, deep heel, but do not push your leg forward as you drive your heel down.

Horse Talk

aids:
Ways the rider communicates with the horse. Natural aids are the hands, voice, seat, and legs; artificial aids include crops and spurs.

posting:
Rising and falling in the saddle as the horse trots. It's easier on the horse's back and easier on the rider as well.

Schaefer is a competent young rider who is looking where she is going.

Clementine is checking with her hand behind her seat to be sure she is not sitting too far back in the saddle. Sitting behind the center of gravity makes it difficult to be in harmony with the horse. Also, even a lightweight rider feels heavy to a horse's kidneys, which are located just behind the saddle.

Here Clementine is sitting correctly on her pony. She sits in the middle of him with her heel under her hip and her elbow in front of her hip. Her eyes are up and her shoulders are back. Her stirrups are perpendicular to the ground and she has her weight in her heels. Her hands are a bit stiff and erect.

CORRECT

She is sitting on the back of the saddle with her feet out in front of her. She can't be in harmony with her pony because she is behind his center of gravity. Her feet are so far away from his ribs that she virtually has no leg on her horse at all. Urging him forward from the leg is next to impossible when her feet are positioned like this.

INCORRECT

Now Clementine's back is rounded. This slouch looks sloppy and is sloppy, as well as ineffective, plus it encourages looking down, not forward. Showing in equitation classes with a rounded back like this would start a performance with at least two strikes against you. A sloppy look can take away a lot from an otherwise good performance.

Her back is too arched and very stiff. This position is also unattractive and ineffective. Some trainers teach an exaggerated arched back, but it can become a problem for a rider's look and performance, for soon the pony senses the stiffness and becomes rigid as well.

People riding horses should look where they are going, both for safety and for a smooth performance. Rounded backs and dropped eyes often go together, but good posture strengthens a mind set to present a good performance.

Correct Leg Position

The leg should hang directly under the rider's hipbone. The rider should sit directly over the stirrup iron so that the leather hangs perpendicular to the ground.

CORRECT

The stirrup is on the ball of Clementine's foot and her heel is down.

INCORRECT

Here her foot is "home" — too far through the stirrup — and her toe is pointing down.

INCORRECT

Clementine is too much on her toe and in danger of losing the stirrup. Also, her leg is too far out in front of her.

INCORRECT

Her weight is too much on the outside of the stirrup.

Good trainers teach their riders "to think like a horse," to develop that elusive quality, "feel" or sensitivity to the animal. Riding a horse well means much more than sitting correctly, though that needs a lot of attention, too, especially in the beginning.

Checking your seat and leg position often works better than trying to hold it every moment. The latter technique creates a stiff, frozen look and no "feel." Feel what your horse is doing under you and adjust your seat and leg position to accommodate him. Aim to be correct but not frozen in the saddle.

The Crop or Whip

A rider should never get on a horse without carrying a crop or whip as an emergency aid only, not as a threat. Beginners should learn, early on, how to carry it correctly so the horse is not alarmed. (With horses, however, no rule is cast in stone. Some horses will just not tolerate a rider carrying a crop.) Except for the occasional slap on the shoulder to straighten the horse, a rider should never use the crop to hit the horse in front of the saddle. Hitting a horse between the ears, or across the neck or face, is cruel and endangers the horse's eyes.

Here Brianne holds the crop correctly, at the end.

Here she is in danger of poking her own eye when she holds the crop in the middle.

The Five Rein Aids

Every rider needs to be able to understand and use the five rein **aids**: the direct rein, indirect rein, bearing rein (or neck rein), leading rein, and pulley rein.

1. The **direct rein** is used for stopping and turning.

2. The **indirect rein** is used against the pony's neck to shift his weight and encourage smooth, balanced turns.

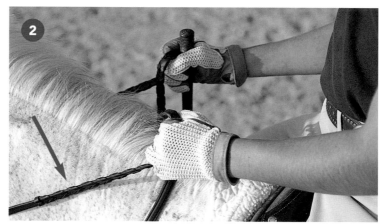

To shorten your reins, bridge them (see page 15), and slide one hand and then the other toward the horse's mouth. Reins can also be shortened by "creeping" the fingers gradually toward the horse's mouth. I prefer the first method, because it is smoother, safer, and more efficient.

The **direct rein** works directly from front to back and is used for stopping and turning. To stop, the rider pulls back on both reins. To turn, she pulls back on only one rein.

The **indirect rein** is used to displace the pony's weight from one side to the other by putting pressure along his neck. In using the indirect rein, you should not raise your hands or cross your reins over the pony's withers. If they do cross over, your reins are too long.

3. The **bearing rein** is used to encourage your pony to turn sharply, particularly in jumping classes, where quick, tight turns are essential.

4. Here, the **leading rein** is pulled away from the pony's neck to "lead" him to the left.

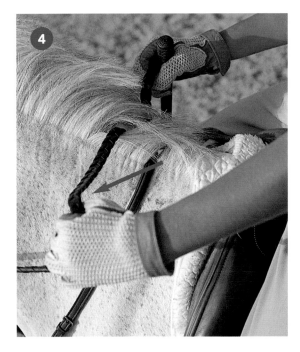

The third rein aid is the **bearing rein.** Western riders call it the neck rein. This rein is applied firmly against the pony's neck to encourage him to turn sharply.

The **leading rein** does just that. It leads the pony to to the left or right. While not seen in the hunter/equitation show ring, it is helpful with green horses and for turning smoothly in jumper classes.

Finally, the **pulley rein** is a very important emergency aid to stop a pony who is running away. Every beginner should know how to use it effectively.

5. For the **pulley rein,** press on the neck with one hand for leverage and pull with all your might with the other hand, pulling the pony in a circle to gain control.

The Posting Trot: The First Big Milestone

You will probably start the **posting** trot on a leadline or longe line. At first you will not get it at all and you will bounce all over the place. Keep trying to feel the rhythm of the trot. It is hard to know how and when to rise. Let the trot toss you up. Suddenly, you get it!

Posting with the motion. Here the angle of Clementine's upper body follows the pony's motion. The rhythm of the pony's trot tosses her gently out of the saddle. There is no effort on the rider's part to throw herself up. Posting with the motion is the more natural post and the correct post for beginner and intermediate riders who need to learn to be in harmony with their horses.

CORRECT

Posting behind the motion. Clementine's angle is very erect. Her back is perpendicular to the pony's back. This angle is suitable for dressage, but not for intermediate hunter seat equitation. As the rider posts, she is driving her pony forward with her seat. Intermediate riders who post behind the motion end up being too stiff and rigid, losing the precious "feel" they should try to develop at that stage. Her leg should be under her, not out in front.

INCORRECT

Posting on the correct (right) diagonal on the track to the left. Clementine is rising as her pony's outside leg is off the ground. (The "outside" is always the side toward the rail. The "inside" is the side toward the center of the ring.) Here the pony is in good balance and she is posting just high enough, rather than exaggerating the post as in the next photograph.

Posting on the wrong (left) diagonal. As the pony's inside leg comes up, Clementine is rising in the saddle while proceeding in a circle to the left. The reason this diagonal is incorrect is that when the pony's inside leg is on the ground, bearing his weight, the rider is sitting in the saddle at that moment and he must bear her weight as well. Also, her reins are too long and her hands are too low, in contrast to the straight line from elbow to mouth, above.

CORRECT

INCORRECT

Mastering Diagonals

The next milestone after learning how to post is mastering your diagonals. When a horse trots, his legs move diagonally: right front and left hind, left front and right hind. When the left front hits the ground and you sit, you are on the left diagonal, and vice versa. Likewise, when the left foot is up, you are up off the saddle. When going in a circle, as in a riding ring, the correct diagonal is governed by the horse's outside leg. ("Outside" is the side toward the rail and "inside" is the side toward the center of the ring.)

The Canter

Once you are fairly secure at the posting trot, it is time to learn to canter. Prepare your horse to canter by putting your outside leg well behind the girth. This will move his hindquarters toward the inside of the ring so that he is properly balanced to strike off on the correct "lead." The correct lead occurs when the inside foreleg seems to step higher — that is, "leads". Once the horse is properly balanced with his hindquarters to the inside, press him strongly with your outside leg to get him to canter.

Cantering on the correct lead. Notice that the pony's inside foreleg leads.

CORRECT

Cantering on the incorrect lead. The pony's outside leg leads.

INCORRECT

Eye Control

Eye control is another major milestone. Beginners find it difficult to know whether or not they are on the correct diagonal or lead. At first you will have to look down over the horse's shoulder to tell which lead or diagonal you are on. Next you can refine the look to a glance. Finally, you will learn to feel and hear whether the lead or diagonal is correct. Feeling is a good habit to develop early.

Focus on Your Destination

Develop the habit of keeping your eyes focused on your destination. Horses have a way of "following your eye." For example, if you want to turn left, look first and then turn your horse. You will find that your turn will be much smoother. Just that little shift in emphasis and weight makes a difference to a sensitive horse. It may feel as though he is reading your mind, but by looking in the direction you want to go, you have telegraphed to him in a subtle way that you intend to make a left turn.

By now you should be riding off the lead- or longe line, and it is time to sharpen your skills. As soon as you are off the leadline or longe line, you need to understand ring rules, which are pretty much universal.

Here Clementine is looking down, a habit that needs to be nipped in the bud. A rider must always look where she is going — just as a car driver looks at the road, not the accelerator. It is first and foremost a safety issue, but riders who keep their heads up will also perform more smoothly, effectively, and confidently.

INCORRECT

Ring Rules

Certain basic ring rules help everyone cope with traffic whether or not the ring is busy. Rings are often crowded because inclement weather forces everyone to ride indoors and/or because after school hours are prime time for riding. However, a ring can feel crowded if you are sharing it with just one person who does not know the basic etiquette of ring riding, and a rider who does not know the rules can really wreak havoc in a crowded ring, whether large or small.

The most important concept to bear in mind when riding in a group or busy ring is to ride "left shoulder to left shoulder," just like in a car on the road. The exception to this is that jumping lessons always have the right of way.

- If you cannot see into the ring, call out "Gate?" or "Door?" to let other riders know you want to come in. They will reply "Okay" if the coast is clear. Avoid cutting riders off or startling their horses.

- Go to the center of the ring (but not in front of any of the jumps!) to mount, dismount, and adjust tack. Also go to the center to put on or remove your clothing and/or your horse's cooler/blanket.

- Once mounted, avoid crowding the other riders. You're at a safe distance behind another horse if you can see his shiny hind horseshoes between your horse's ears. You will then be two to three horse lengths behind him — well out of kicking range.

- Traffic rules are simple: Pass left shoulder to left shoulder — always — except when someone jumping a course shouts "Rail."

- Jumping horses always have the right of way. As you ride around the ring, listen up to know which pattern of fences the teacher wants the horse and rider to jump, so you can stay out of the way.

Schooling on the Flat

Kathryn is competing in a 1st Level dressage test. Her position and turnout is very correct and her pony is well-balanced. Notice that dressage riders traditionally ride with a longer stirrup.

Most riding teachers borrow the traditional letters from the dressage arena, where dressage riders practice "haute école." The basic exercises taught in early lessons will stand in good stead for any rider who chooses to proceed to dressage. For the rest of us, the letters help us organize our daily ride, as they provide points to ride to. Because many rings have these letters, even a strange ring has an aura of familiarity about it.

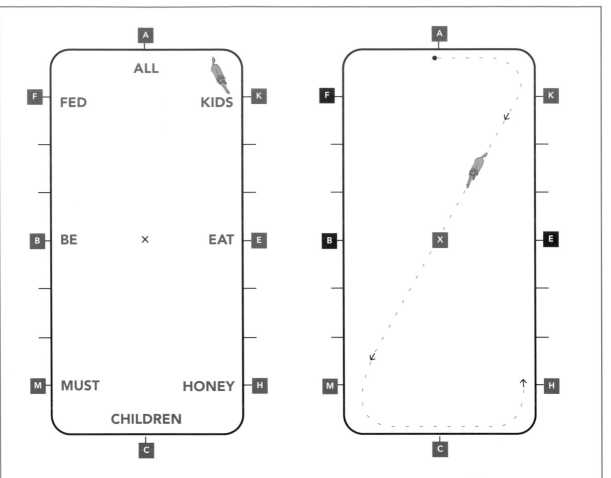

The standard dressage arena is 66 feet x 132 feet, but although ring size will vary from stable to stable, the letters will always be in the same order. The placement of the letters around the ring seems random; no one has a good explanation as to why they are where they are. There are various sentences to help us remember which letter goes where. Proceeding clockwise from "A" (see illustration above left), my favorite is "All Kids Eat Honey; Children Must Be Fed."

The diagrams here and on pages 39–43 feature suggested exercises to practice, first at the walk, later at the trot, and then at the canter. Using the letters will help you learn to keep your horse straight on the straightaway and nicely bent on the turns. Letters force the rider to use her eyes to look where she is going, and focusing on the destination will help her reach it.

A ring with letters encourages riders to be precise; for example, to trot the diagonal pattern A-K-X-M-C-H (shown in pink above) is not as easy as it looks. Even world class dressage riders must be very attentive to do the required exercise at the designated letter.

Work on Transitions

Begin with an ordinary trot to warm up. Don't be too demanding in the first few minutes. Trot on a long rein but not one that's too loose.

Now work on transitions through the trot (sitting, ordinary, and strong) on circles and straight lines. The sitting trot is slower than the ordinary trot, and the rider sits rather than posts. Sitting to the trot is not as easy as it looks. Relax your back and keep the trot slow. The ordinary trot is 6 to 7 miles an hour. The strong trot is an accelerated, extended version of the ordinary trot. Horses need to practice transitions from one trot to another in order to develop proper rhythm, balance, and, most important, obedience to the rider's aids. Be sure the horse is straight on the lines and that the arc of his body is parallel to the arc of the circles and turns.

After working through transitions at the trot, move on to the canter. A beginner usually uses the outside rein and outside leg to urge her horse into a canter. Later, these lateral aids are replaced by diagonal aids: An inter-mediate rider uses the inside indirect rein to bend the horse slightly in the direction she wants to go, accompa-nied by pressure from her outside leg behind the girth. A gentle nudge with the outside leg before you actually ask for the canter will shift your horse's hindquarter to the inside. He will be able to pick up the correct lead, and the nudge will get his attention as well.

Practice transitions between the ordinary and the strong canter. The ordinary canter is the horse's normal canter; the strong canter is slightly faster, but is not a full gallop. Cantering at different speeds teaches the horse to obey the rider's aids. Later, the rider will be able to adjust the length of the stride as the pony approaches jumps. A horse that lengthens and shortens his stride easily has a tremendous advantage over one that does not. Some horses are naturally quite adjustable; others need constant training.

Developing sound basics from the begin-ning makes achieving excellence later much more likely. Concen-trate on developing a good position and main-taining proper control of your horse.

The next step is to practice transitions from one gait to another, including the halt and the back. Be sure to use both reins and both legs for all transitions, upward (faster) and downward (slower). Practicing transitions (that is, going faster and slower at each gait) is the best exercise for making the horse longitudinally obedient.

Halts and Half-Halts

For halts, close both your leg and your hand to keep your horse immobile and straight. Stretch your back up as you close the leg and the hand. Hold his mouth gently with the reins and keep a little leg on him. As soon as he responds, ease the pressure on your reins so that he is rewarded for his obedience. Then he will not overreact and back up.

The half-halt is exactly that. The rider asks the horse to halt and, just as he is about to halt, rides him forward. The half-halt, though barely visible, is a simultaneous, coordinated action of the legs, seat, and hands to get the horse's attention and balance him before executing various movements or transitions to slower or faster paces.

In the half-halt, the rider first asks for a halt. Stretch your back up and close the legs and hands.

Then, just as he is about to halt, ride your horse forward by easing the pressure on the reins.

A rider who takes and takes but never rewards the horse's proper response soon will have an uncooperative horse on her hands.

The half-halt engages the horse's hindquarters and therefore lightens his forehand and his balance in general. Repeated half-halts are effective when the horse is too sluggish and when he goes too fast. It is a quick, short gathering of the horse, an assertive signal from the rider to the horse to pay attention and obey commands.

Less experienced riders tend to "rein back" their horses by using only their hands. More advanced riders close their legs as they close their hands to achieve a more balanced rein back. As the horse yields and backs a step or two, soften the hand. Don't continually choke him. This principle of rewarding the horse's correct response is an important one in the art of horsemanship.

Whenever a horse reacts positively to the rider's aids, he must be rewarded, or soon he will not react to them at all. And who can blame him? Why should he behave if there is no reward? Ask for a few steps at a time at first, and be sure to keep the horse straight. Don't ask him to back every time you halt or he will learn this as his lesson and run backward at every halt, which is a major disobedience.

A

F   K

← 20m (65') →

The volté

B   X   E

M   H

C

In dressage, the **volté** is a circle always 20 meters (65 feet) in diameter. Practice keeping your circles perfectly round.

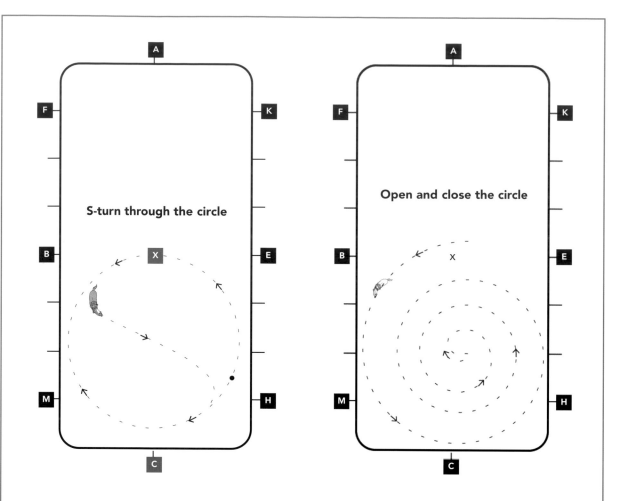

S-turn through the circle

Open and close the circle

The **S-turn through the circle** is a good way to practice changing direction. Then **open and close the circle** at the trot and the canter.

From Circles to Serpentines

Practicing circles at all gaits is an exercise in precision. Be sure the circles are entirely round and not lopsided. The favorite exercise, a **volté,** is a circle 20 meters (65 feet) in diameter. Circles are also good for settling a fresh horse and for controlling a rambunctious one.

The **S-turn through the circle,** as from X to C, is one way to change direction: bending, then straightening one or two strides, and then bending in the other direction.

Next, do the **open and close the circle** exercise at the trot and canter, using the same midpoint to teach the horse to stay in the "frame," between hands and legs. This exercise makes the rider deal with two potential problems: cutting in and bulging out.

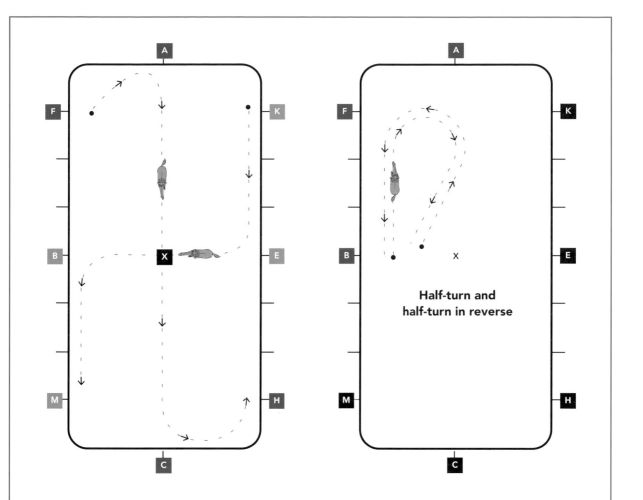

**Half-turn and
half-turn in reverse**

For other ways to change direction besides crossing the diagonal, ride **F**-A-**X**-C-H (shown in pink and black) down the length of the ring, or K-E-**X**-B-M (shown in green and black) across the short side of the ring.

Next, practice changes of direction across the diagonal. In your ring, for example, ride F-A-**X**-C-H, or across the short side of the ring, K-E-**X**-B-M. Again, be sure the horse is straight on lines and bent around your inside leg on the turns.

The next exercise is **half-turns and half-turns in reverse,** at all gaits. For example, to do a half-turn, proceed along B, turn at F, pushing your horse toward the rail with your inside leg as you return to B (but never over center line A-**X**-C). For half-turns in reverse, proceed from B toward A (again not over center line A-**X**-C) and then left at F and finally again past B. Changing direction develops a horse's lateral suppleness just as transitions in pace develop his longitudinal suppleness.

Concentrate on neat, prompt departs into the canter from the walk. The horse's head should be bent slightly to the inside as you apply the outside leg, gently at first to make sure his hindquarters are engaged (i.e., toward the inside), and then more firmly to ask him to strike off at the canter. The amount of leg pressure depends on the horse: Sensitive horses need a light squeeze; dull ones, a kick — or even a slap with the crop if they ignore the kick. As a rider gets to know his horse, he learns to sense how much pressure to apply. This is the beginning of developing "feel."

Encourage a free, ordinary, unhurried walk. Allow the horse to stretch his head and neck. Use good judgment about giving him a break when working intensively on the flat. Ride and then relax.

Novice riders should learn to perform the **turn on the forehand**, the first exercise in lateral movement for young horses and young riders. When you turn on the forehand, do it one step at a time, not hurriedly. Your eyes should be up and your heels down. Hold your horse's head gently with the reins. Your inside leg should be on the girth, with the active outside leg pressing behind the girth to push his hindquarters around his stationary forehand.

Another good exercise is to ride **broken lines** and **serpentines** at all gaits. A broken line can be ridden, for example, from C and H toward X, then to K and A. This is a good exercise for practicing eye control: At H look toward X; as you reach X, shift your eyes to K.

Serpentine loops should match precisely in length and width. Starting at C, proceed past M across the ring to an imaginary point between E and H; at E

Ten minutes of concentrated riding is better than 30 minutes of purposeless meandering around the ring. Do not work your horse constantly; give him a little break every 10 to 15 minutes.

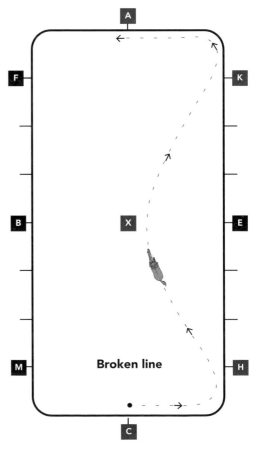

Broken line

turn left across X and right again at B; halfway between B and F, turn right toward another imaginary point between E and K; proceed past K to A. The horse should be perfectly straight on the lines and nicely bent around your inside leg on the turns.

Practice a **figure-eight** at the trot and canter. Make nice round circles, holding the horse out on the circle and looking in to the center point for accuracy. The "focal point" (A) is on the rail; the "center point," where the change is made, is about 18 feet in from the rail, a little over the radius of the intended circle.

At the canter, do simple or flying changes. A simple change can be executed through either the trot or the walk. (See page 45 for an explanation of flying changes.) If the horse anticipates change, walk a few

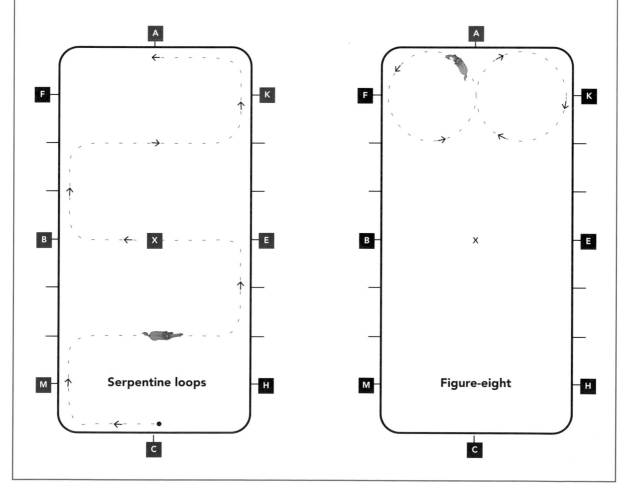

Serpentine loops

Figure-eight

steps or halt four or five seconds between changes to increase his obedience to your directions.

Leg yielding is another basic exercise to teach the horse to be obedient to the lateral aids. It supples him and prepares him for more advanced lateral movements such as the shoulder-in. Leg yielding involves bending the horse around the active leg, which pushes him away from the side where the leg is active. It can be done on a straight line, on a turn, on a circle, or across the diagonal. At the turns, the rider can apply the inside indirect rein with an active inside leg, pressing the horse away from the inside of the ring. Keep the horse moving forward and prevent — with the outside leg — his haunches from swinging too much to the outside.

Flying lead changes are next. The horse's body must be completely straight before the rider asks for a change. To teach him flying changes, shift hands to the outside of the turn to displace his weight from his inside shoulder to his outside haunch, meanwhile holding his hindquarters in with the outside leg as well. Then ask for the change with a strong outside leg. Do not let him increase his pace as you ask for the change. Use the rail or the wall of the ring to force the change and prevent the horse from getting away from you.

At horse shows now, perfect flying lead changes on course are absolutely essential, even at the beginner and intermediate levels, so take the time to learn to do them correctly and to teach your horse. Keep after him until he does them perfectly whenever asked. He may very well get upset until he understands what you want and has the

In the **leg yield,** apply the inside rein and inside leg and use the outside leg to prevent the horse's haunches from swinging out. Both hands and both legs control the whole horse.

Be patient and use good judgment. A frantic horse cannot learn, so keep it simple and keep him calm. Finish the day with something the horse does well.

coordination to do it. Don't be deterred by his getting in a flap; on the other hand, do not drill him until he is frantic.

Include simple changes with emphasis on straightness to help him understand the process and stay calm. The flying change should always be introduced and practiced at first under your trainer's supervision, for it is a difficult and important exercise.

As you are working your horse on the flat remember that he is an animal, not a machine. When you start, give him a chance to loosen up before you demand absolute obedience. Walk first for a few minutes, unless the weather is freezing cold, then trot right away. A brisk trot in large circles and around the ring is a good way to start the day. During the course of your flatwork, take a break now and then. Your teammate relies on your good judgment. Let him walk on a loose rein, relax, and stretch his neck. He is not a bicycle, a tennis racket, or a football; he is your friend. Keep it that way.

This shows a **flying lead change** from the right lead to the left lead. First, shift the hands to the outside of the turn to displace the horse's weight from his inside shoulder to his outside haunch, meanwhile holding his hindquarters in with the outside leg.

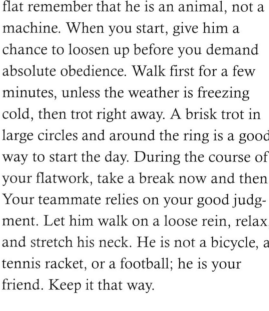

Ask for the change with a strong outside leg.

Here the horse's weight is shifting from the right foreleg to the left.

At the end of your work, let your horse relax, and if your teacher gives you the go-ahead, maybe even take him for a bareback stroll. Obviously, you need to have developed a secure seat, and you want a quiet horse before you embark on a bareback ride. **Safety and good sense must always come first.**

After a strenuous lesson, sometimes a relaxed bareback ride is in order. Here Haley's pony wears his halter and two lead ropes, instead of a bridle. (This is recommended only for very quiet ponies.)

The pony convinces Haley that he would really like to have a few mouthfuls of grass.

Work on the Longe Line

The longe line is an important piece of equipment for young riders to know how to use correctly. In the very beginning it is a handy and safe way to start riding. Intermediate riders should learn early on how to longe a horse, for it is the quickest and safest method for working down a fresh horse.

If the wind comes up or the weather turns suddenly cold, quiet "foolproof" horses and ponies can make liars of us all. They too can buck and spook. Anytime a horse or pony has had several days of rest, be on guard. If he is too fresh, longe him for a few minutes instead of letting him dump you. In the beginning, have someone experienced help you longe him or longe him for you. Don't let other riders deter you from your plan to longe a fresh pony with their accusations of "Chicken." Tell them, "Better a live chicken than a hurt or dead duck."

Pony back talk! A pony or horse that wants to buck like this needs a five- to ten-minute gallop on the longe line before a rider climbs aboard. Even the very best ponies can get frisky, especially when it's cold and windy.

Here is how to attach the longe line to the bridle. Run the line through the bit on the horse's left side, over his head, and . . .

. . . attach the snap to the bit on the right (outside). Now you are ready to longe him to the left. To longe him to the right, run the line through the bit on his right side over his head and snap it on the left side.

Another important function of the longe line is that it enables the rider to practice her position and to develop her ability to be "tight" on the horse. Sometimes the teacher will give you a "longe line lesson," a necessary but always dreaded affair, as it is difficult to ride without reins and/or stirrups. In our barn the riders often take turns longeing (and teaching) each other.

First make sure the horse or pony is quiet enough. If in doubt, it is always safest to start a rider on the longe line with both reins and stirrups. First tie up the reins and then remove the stirrups. After a while, the rider can practice without reins and stirrups both. Besides the usual walk, trot (sitting and posting), and canter, there

A one-rein snaffle bit is the easiest to use for longeing with a bridle.

are several good exercises to practice as the rider gets more secure.

Eventually a small jump can be included. Begin with just a rail on the ground. Set it perpendicular to a fence line so the horse cannot run out on the far side. Again, start jumping with reins and stirrups, and remove them when the rider is getting tight enough to jump without them.

Working without stirrups on the flat, over fences, and especially on the longe line is the best exercise for strengthening your legs and developing a secure seat. Ride without stirrups as often as possible, always being careful that the horse is quiet enough.

Here, Brianne prepares for some longeing exercises. For work on the longe line without stirrups, pull down the stirrup buckles and cross them over the pommel of the saddle, so there is no lumpy buckle under the rider's leg.

Next, snap the knotted reins to the saddle.

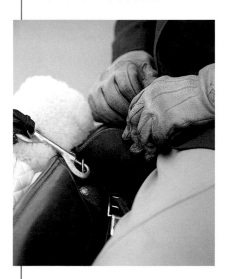

1. Brianne holds herself by securely grasping the pommel (front) of the saddle with her outside hand and the cantle (back) with her inside hand, thereby positioning herself to look in the direction she is going around the circle.

2. Now she is totally dependent on the legs. She has put her hands on her hips and her feet in the stirrups.

3. Next she spreads her arms . . .

4. . . . and rotates facing the inside of the circle, then the outside, gripping tightly with her legs all the while.

After a few weeks or months, you will start to feel more and more that you and your horse are partners, a team of two. Even if you ride a different horse in each lesson, this feeling of togetherness is what makes riding horses different from all other sports. From the very beginning you want to develop the habit of gaining rapport with your horse. Try to understand both his frame of mind and his point of view. Then figure out how to persuade him, or coerce him if necessary, to do what you want him to do. Be firm, but not rough, as you coax him. Work on the flat is the foundation for good riding, whether for pleasure or for competition, because diligent flatwork is also the foundation for the horse's obedience to the rider's aids.

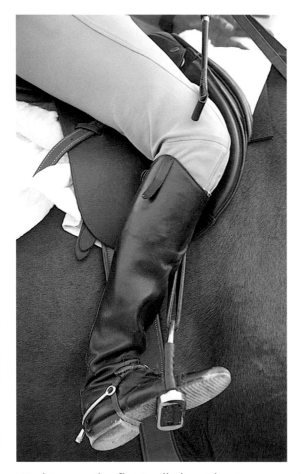 

Working on the flat is all about having a good leg, no matter what level you are riding at.

Rewards of Hard Work

Amy Lowrey is a hard-working riding student whose career as a horse-woman is developing nicely. She is fortunate that her aunt Kim has a thriving horse business and early on taught Amy to ride well. Kim provided nice ponies for her to ride and show and in return Amy works hard around the farm. As a junior in college, she placed second in the USET (United States Equestrian Team) Finals coached by Peter Lutz.

Youngsters whose parents cannot afford to buy horses can find other ways to support their riding lessons — usually working in and around the barn, cleaning stalls and tack, and saddling and grooming horses. There are countless examples of great riders who have never owned a horse. You must be energetic, patient, and, above all, persistent.

CHAPTER 3

Riding over Jumps

"One invariable rule that cannot be too strongly stressed is that a horse must always be straight at his fences."

— LYDIA FLEITMAN

Once you feel fairly secure at the trot and canter, it is time to start a little jumping. My feeling is that knowing diagonals and leads is not totally necessary at this stage. Your teacher may not agree on this point, and you should always abide by his or her program. The instructor who is responsible for your progress and your safety should always be the ultimate authority.

Horse Talk

cavaletti:
A series of parallel poles or rails placed on the ground or on low supports.

crest release:
A maneuver in which the rider rests her hands on top of the horse's neck (the crest) for support during a jump.

Jumping Step-by-Step

Jumping is not just about the jump itself. There is a sequence of steps. The horse and rider must approach the jump properly, take the jump correctly, land well, and immediately organize themselves for the next jump. The rider's position and aids direct the horse's balance, rhythm, and track.

Here is a simplified description of things to keep in mind as you begin. Throughout the jump, the rider keeps strong weight in her heels. As the horse approaches the jump, the rider takes the half-seat position (see below). As the horse lifts off, the rider supports and stabilizes herself with the crest release (see page 57). When the horse lands, the rider looks ahead to the next jump.

Learning the Half-Seat

Before actually starting to jump fences, you should be able to hold the half-seat at the trot and canter. The half-seat, or two-point position, is also called the jumping position. It is an excellent exercise for strengthening your legs and deepening your heels even if you have no intention of ever jumping.

Listen carefully and trust your teacher's judgment.

This girl is not posting, but rather holding her half-seat, also known as the jumping position, or "two-point."

Here, Clementine holds her half-seat as she canters over a rail on the ground. Notice that her lower leg has slipped a bit and her toes point out too much. She needs to close her hip angle a little, as she is rather erect here.

If I were to choose one exercise to improve a rider's position and strength, the half-seat at all gaits is it. Practice it frequently, especially in your beginning years of riding.

First, shorten your stirrups one hole from where you have them on the flat. You will be more secure with a shorter stirrup. Next, shorten your reins and rise so that your seat does not quite touch the saddle. Your upper body should be inclined slightly forward. Your weight should rest totally in your heels, which you press down to absorb the shock of the horse's movement and/or jump. Practice the half-seat at all three gaits: walk, trot, and canter.

Only when a rider has developed a strong leg and is secure in the jump should she start practicing a "following hand," first over low, easy jumps. The following hand is just that: ideally, it follows the horse's mouth as he jumps. This is an advanced skill. Intermediate riders should still do the crest release to avoid supporting themselves in the air by pulling on the horse's mouth until their legs are strong enough.

Learning the Crest Release

When it's time to begin jumping lessons, the rider usually starts by trotting between specific standards and over rails (called **cavaletti**) on the ground. The most important thing to practice at this point is the crest release, so that when the horse jumps, he has the freedom to use his head and neck.

The **crest release** (resting the hands halfway up the crest of the horse's neck) helps beginners stay in the middle of their horses, not falling ahead or behind them. Later, when the rider is completely secure, she can practice a following hand. A loose rider typically falls back over the top of the jump and pulls on the horse's mouth. Constant jerks in the mouth will discourage even the most courageous and generous horse.

When you are starting out, reach up and grab a piece of mane to make sure the thrust of the jump doesn't unseat you or cause you to fall back and bang your horse in the mouth. Once you have mastered the release trotting over a single rail, do a line of two rails at least 60 feet apart, first at the trot and then at the canter. Keep practicing: Feel his mouth, release. Feel, release. Feel . . .

Even as an intermediate rider when I first saw him in a local Pony Club horse show, Peter Lutz had mastered the following hand, thanks to his long strong legs and an extraordinary "feel." A proper following hand allows the rider to maintain contact with his horse during the flight of the jump.

While approaching the rail (and later the jump) in the half-seat, feel your pony's mouth on the approach, rest hands on the crest for the jump, then feel his mouth again on landing. Rest your hands firmly on his neck to support yourself — or if necessary, grab some mane.

Cantering over rails on the ground is the best way to simulate jumping jumps, as everything but the flight of the jump can be practiced: the half-seat, the approach, the release, and the departure.

Usually the next step after trotting and cantering rails on the ground is to start trotting small cross rails: first a single X, then two, and finally a little pattern or course. (See the diagrams on pages 66, 70, and 72 for some basic patterns and courses.) Your teacher will know when you are ready to canter to the jumps and finally to jump a little higher. Jumps need not be high for practicing basic skills. Some trainers encourage riders to practice cantering rails and low jumps between lessons. Others prefer their students to jump only under supervision. Here again, you must respect your teacher's judgment.

Clementine does a nice job over this cross rail. Her eyes are up and her position is just fine. I especially like her nice deep heel. She could close her hip angle a little as she does so well in the photo below.

CORRECT

Good form for both pony and rider. Clementine's eyes are up, her weight is in her heels, and her crest release has become a "following hand." She is in the middle of her pony, neither ahead of him nor behind him.

CORRECT

Here Clementine is standing too erect and is over the pommel of the saddle. She needs to drop into her heels more and close her hip angle.

(Bottom left) Brianne is right in the middle of her horse where she belongs, as he is about to engage his hindquarters to leave the ground.

(Bottom right) Here Brianne is "climbing up his neck." Her body is way ahead of the horse's and her leg has slipped back. Because she has thrown her weight forward, the horse has lost his form and is hanging his knees instead of tucking them up under his chin.

The Approach

What makes a good jump is a proper approach, with the correct balance, rhythm, and track. The horse should carry himself lightly to the jump with his weight evenly distributed on all four legs, not leaning on his forehand and the rider's hands. The rhythm of his trot or canter should be medium. If it's too fast, he will arrive too soon, leaving out strides or "chipping in" (adding strides at the last minute); if too slow, he will again add last-minute

strides. Likewise, his stride should be medium, not too long and flat or too short and choppy, so the rider can regulate the stride to create a nice jump. The track is also important; the horse must be straight and jump the middle of the fence, neither cutting in nor falling out on the turns.

The Landing

When you land over the jump, it is important to know what you will do next. You have many options. One is "to stop on a line" — that is, to halt promptly, smoothly, and straight, facing directly away from the rail or jump. A second option is to turn left or right afterward and then halt. Another plan is to circle left or right and then halt. Any of these ideas is appropriate, but be sure you develop the habit to have a plan when you land after a jump. Later, when you are jumping courses and the fences are coming up quickly, you will be glad you have that habit of planning before you land over a jump.

Brianne is holding her half-seat on landing, with her weight correctly in her heels.

CORRECT

Brianne is ducking off to the side instead of looking between the horse's ears toward the next jump, or wherever she plans to go after landing.

Here Brianne has been "left behind," hitting her horse in the back and in the mouth.

The Importance of Good Flatwork

You will soon notice the tremendous value of good flatwork as you begin your jumping career. Riders and horses both must have a sound background in flatwork if they intend to become competent over jumps.

For instance, as mentioned earlier, nowadays in the show ring, flying changes are absolutely necessary even in short-stirrup cross-rail classes if you want to be at the top of the class. Some horses do them almost automatically, but even so, you will need to know exactly how to balance a horse so he can execute the flying change properly.

Kelsey is demonstrating excellent use of her eyes. She is on course at a horse show and as she rounds the turn, her attention is fixed on the next jump. The pony's ears indicate that he is reading her directions. Looking early is the first step in "seeing the jumps."

Seeing the Jumps

A good rider looks ahead to find the place where the horse will leave the ground, not too close and not too far from the jump (usually about 6 feet from the base of the fence). Some riders seem to "see the jumps" more easily than others. This is because they look ahead to the next jump, feel their horse's balance and rhythm, and are aware of the best track to the jump. If the balance, rhythm, and track are correct, the jump will be at least decent, if not wonderful.

Finding Your Balance

Young riders must learn to tune in to their horse's balance. Is he on his forehand? Is he drifting to the left or right? He needs to be straight and jump the middle of the fence. You are the one to guide him there.

Setting the Rhythm

Rhythm is more than just fast and slow. It is a matter of RPM as well as MPH. The horse's stride needs to be lively, but not too long or too short. As one good old horseman once explained to me, "As you go around a course, try to keep him at 35, then you can go up to 40 or down to 30 without major adjustments. If you go at 30, to get him up to 40 will be a project. So will getting him from 40 quickly back to 30." The numbers are not as important as the concept: Go for the medium speed and then you can move up or down as needed.

Correcting the Track

Of the three important elements — balance, rhythm, and track — the easiest to make correct is the track itself. As you come around the corner of the ring to the jump, make sure the horse does not cut the turn or do the opposite — drift out on the turn. In other words, he should not fall in or fall out, but instead follow the arc of the circle around to the jump.

Remember where the in-gate is. Every horse at least thinks about falling out toward the in-gate as he goes past and falling in on the far end of the ring. Some horses just think about it, but most try to do it! If you forget where the in-gate is, you will definitely have trouble figuring out how to ride the track.

The most important rule for those who do not "see the distance" is to be patient and wait until you do. Don't grab at the distance you "think" you see, for you will alarm your horse with last-minute spurring. Nor should you break up his stride with rough hands grabbing at his mouth. Sit still and wait it out. The jump is not going anywhere, and you will get to it eventually, so just be patient. Sit still, keep your hands still, and let the horse jump when he gets to the fence.

If you have developed the habit of organizing when you land over a jump and go into the turn, then as you come out of the turn you can relax and allow the horse to show you the distance. (Related distances between the jumps will be dealt with later.) Easy to say, but not all that easy to do. Years of practice on many different horses will probably help!

Schooling over Low Jumps

Trotting fences discourages too much anticipation by horse and rider. The rider may hold the half-seat as he trots the fence or may post the trot, sitting only the last couple of strides. With horses that need a lot of leg to hold them together, it may be better if the rider sits the trot all the way to the jump. I start nearly all sessions with trotting low fences.

Here Clementine needs to close her hip angle just a little. Otherwise her position is correct. Her trainer, Peter Lutz, is in the background.

Setting Up a Schooling Course

The diagram below represents a good basic schooling course for young riders. The pattern is based on a typical jumping arena 75' x 100'. All these jumps should be constructed so they can be jumped from either direction for maximum use of the pattern.

An elaborate course is not necessary for practicing simple exercises over jumps. Any of the jumps can be jumped individually. The diagram below offers numerous possibilities for lessons and for dozens of patterns to practice. A rider with horse sense usually begins by trotting and then cantering the simplest single fences, jumping them toward the in-gate, "home," the first time. (Always remember the horse's point of view!)

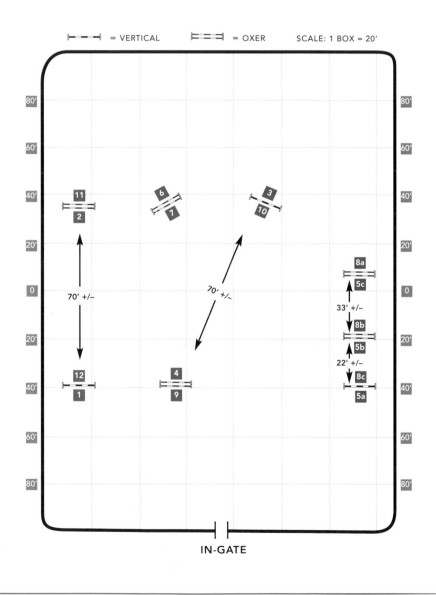

A **vertical** jump involves height without width. It has one pair of standards (supports) and a single element that can consist of poles, gates, planks, or walls, alone or in combination. An **oxer** is a spread jump with a front (the take-off side of the obstacle) and a back (landing side) element that are constructed either to be equal in height or with the front element slightly lower than the back. Normally only a single pole is used for the back element.

— from *101 Jumping Exercises for Horse & Rider* by Linda L. Allen

Three Basic Jumping Exercises

Departures from the fence are as important as [...]es, so upon landing you should incorporate one of [...] three following exercises:

1. Stop on a line. Then turn on the forehand. Concentrate on straightness.
2. Shift hands to the outside, then press the horse out toward the rail with your inside leg as you bend him around that leg and hold him with the outside leg. Keep the horse on the track you want, always using both reins and both legs. Halt at the end of the ring, or make a circle before halting. Halt if he is very strong. Circle if he needs to organize himself.
3. Shift hands to the outside, ask for a flying change if necessary, and continue around the turn holding out and looking in toward the next jump.

Practice holding the half-seat — between jumps as well as over the jumps. An especially effective exercise is to hold the half-seat through a series of gymnastics. Alternate trotting and cantering fences with halts, turns, and lines after the jump to reinforce the horse's obedience to your aids.

When schooling, see that the horse remains ridable and obedient between jumps. If he gets too fast or misses a change of lead, circle him. If he then gets strong after the change, circle again until he settles. Circling is a wonderful settling device before and after the jump. Circling works best when a horse gets too fast, especially a sensitive horse. Pulling up abruptly may rattle him.

On the other hand, don't use the circle to indulge yourself as the rider and director. If you are late organizing upon landing over a jump, it is tempting just to circle rather than to be prompt yourself. Don't let yourself fall into this habit of circling because you fail to organize yourself and your horse promptly.

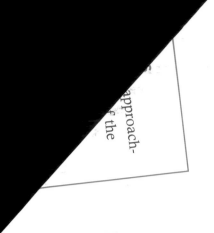

Use the jumping arena diagram on page 66 to develop some gymnastic exercises. After a few simple jumps, the gymnastic on the right side of the ring is a good exercise (8A, 8B, 8C, reverse to 5A, 5B, 5C). Start with it very low — cross rails even — and jump it from both directions at the canter. Gradually make it higher and wider: 2' or 2'6" for ponies, 3' or 3'3" high and wide at the most for horses. After mastering the gymnastic, add fences 6 and 2, and perhaps finally the line 3 and 4.

Working on Stride Control

When you ride a line like that of fences 1 and 2, for example, your horse will canter a certain number of strides between those two jumps. For schooling, the distance between those jumps should be somewhat short of a multiple of 12 feet. Courses for novice riders are

Schaefer has obviously done her homework, for at the show her pony is jumping straight and true.

usually set on the 12-foot stride. Allowing six feet for landing and six feet for takeoff, if the distance is 70 to 72 feet, then your horse will canter five strides between those two jumps. Most ponies will canter six strides.

First, practice adding a stride. In a slow-collected canter, jump into the line and fit six strides in the 70-foot line. Again, you will find the exercise easier going away from "home," the in-gate, and when jumping in over a vertical, so practice that first. Next work on jumping in over the oxer; make sure you add the extra stride early, rather than at the last minute in front of the vertical. Once you master fitting in the six strides going both directions, practice alternating five and six strides: six up and five back, then five up and six back. S-turns on the ends are useful for turning yourself around.

Whether these strides will be forward or steady depends on the horse's natural length of stride and/or his temperament. The five strides will be forward for a lazy and/or short-strided horse. That means when you land over fence 1, you will need to close your legs and urge him forward to fence 2. If your horse has a long stride and/or a keen temperament, the five strides will be the right length, so just keep cantering — but don't hurry. If you jump the line backward, over oxer 11, for a keen and/or long-strided horse the five strides to fence 12 will be easy. However, you will have to slow him down. The oxer will carry him farther into the line than a vertical jump will, and you are going toward "home," so you will get there much more easily. For a final school before a show you may want your distances to be the full 12-foot striding or 72 feet here.

Understanding the horse's point of view is often a matter of common sense. The same five-stride distance rides differently, depending on when it occurs in the course. For some horses, 70 feet will be a bit long if it is the first line of the course, but if it is the last line of the course, it will ride short for most.

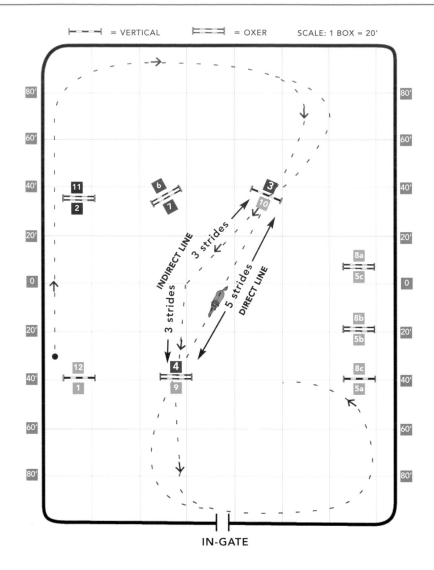

There are two types of
lines, direct and indirect,
with many variations in
between, depending on
the horse's stride and the
size of the jumps. This
exercise encourages
practice of both types.

Finding Your Line

To ride a **direct** line (see diagram above) from fence 3 to
4, you must "look for your line" — that is, look for fence
4 beyond fence 3. When you see fence 4 between the
standards of 3, you have your direct line. Always seek
your line first and then the distance. Look for your
distance to 3 and continue directly to 4 in five strides.

If you want to ride an **indirect** or **broken** line from 3
to 4, jump and ride straight three strides, turn a bit left,
and ride three more strides. Practice doing the direct five
strides and the indirect six strides. Both are correct, and

you should be comfortable doing both exercises.

Once you have mastered the **3** to **4** line, work back and forth over **3** and **4**. Again, if you are doing a direct line, you need to line up the second jump as you come around the turn to the first. Jump across the first jump into the line and across the second jump as well. Also practice the indirect line between **6** and **4**. Jump each fence as it is built and add a stride.

The **6/7** jump alone presents several interesting possibilities. Cantering up the length of the ring away from the in-gate, be sure you ride right up to the **7** jump. Horses back off jumps alone at the far end of the ring away from the in-gate. Jumping it the **6** way, on the left lead, enables you to practice jumping off a short turn. To practice a short turn on the right lead, look early around the **2/11** jump to find your distance.

Serpentines

To do the **serpentine exercise,** (see diagram on page 72) cut the ring in half and jump in the pattern of fences **11, 7, 3,** and **5C**: jump, turn, jump, turn, jump, turn, jump. There is little space in this exercise, so you must be sure to use all the areas that are available to you. Do not let your horse anticipate and cut in to the jump as you round the turn. Stay on the track and keep your rhythm/pace. Short, tight turns will cause your horse to slow down, so make sure he keeps going, but at the same time do not rush the turn.

Even in a very simple and straightforward course, like the one on page 72, countless options exist. The best way to become a good rider is to experiment with the choices. The jumps need not be high for beginner and intermediate riders; a maximum of 3'3" is plenty, and for most, 2' is enough. Regardless of the height of the fences, the exercises, the "problems," and the questions asked are essentially the same. Master them at 2' or 3' and you will someday find 4' or 5' courses easy.

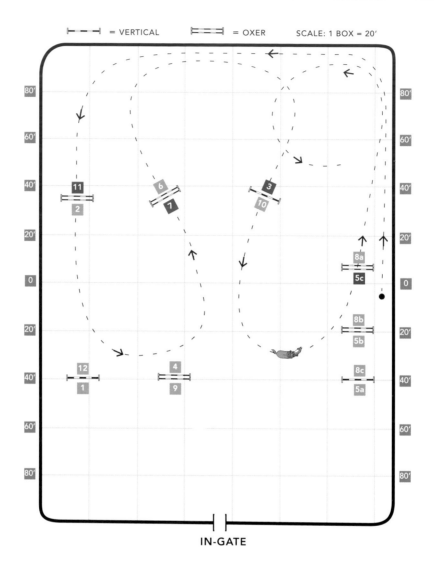

= VERTICAL   = OXER   SCALE: 1 BOX = 20'

IN-GATE

A serpentine is an exercise for practicing jumping off a shorter turn. Use all the area available in order to jump the fence straight and make a good turn afterwards. This is a good exercise for hot horses.

Take It Slow and Keep It Low

Riders and trainers alike must remember not to "use up" their horses in their zeal to become more proficient. Landing over larger jumps takes its toll on any horse's legs. A viable compromise for riders yearning to improve with horses that do not need to make 1,000 jumps is to work over rails on the ground in various patterns and to hop over patterns of very low jumps. Everything is the same with a rail on the ground or a low jump except the actual flight over a large jump, so lines, angles, and turns

This pony is making an extravagant jump, and his rider is right with him!

There is an old saying among horsemen that for every fence a horse jumps, there is one less at the end. Don't cruise carelessly over fences. Make every jump count.

can be mastered without using up and abusing the horse. Kids often have fun jumping courses on foot, another way to practice without using up your horse.

The Benefits of Bareback

Meanwhile, keep working on your basics. You will enjoy riding more and more as you gain experience. One activity that develops basics is riding bareback. Be sure your teacher approves. Riding bareback unsupervised can be dangerous, so make sure you have the go-ahead before you discard your saddle.

Riding bareback helps you develop muscles to hold yourself on the horse, so you will develop more "feel." It is easier to feel what your horse is doing when there is no saddle between you and him. But more than anything, riding bareback is fun!

Bareback riding is good for developing a tight seat. Haley's hands are well placed and here her legs are hanging down straight. Bareback riders can also practice pulling up their knees and putting down their heels to imitate their position in the saddle.

Haley has found a little jump to pop over. All this bareback work is fun, and makes for a better rider at the same time.

Jumping Dos & Don'ts

This boy demonstrates a good crest release and a nice deep heel but is a bit farther up the horse's neck than he needs to be.

This girl's eyes and position are correct, but her heels could be deeper.

Brianne is demonstrating good form. She has a nice following hand, but she is a bit ahead and her leg has slipped back a little. All in all, though, very tidy.

Here Brianne demonstrates a crest release and basic good form.

Renick's position is quite good and she is using the crest release. Her eyes are directed straight ahead. Her lower leg has slipped back just a bit, but her heel is down. She is "in the middle" of her pony — just where she should be.

Clementine's hands and upper body are just right. Her leg has slipped a bit and her heel could be deeper. I wish this pony had a better expression. Sour looks do not help.

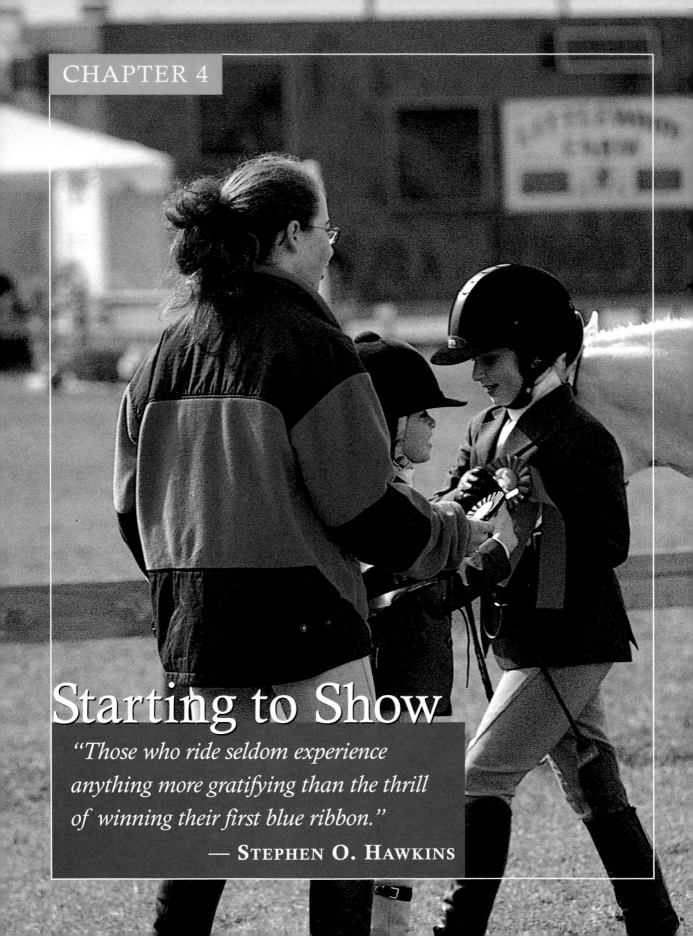

CHAPTER 4

Starting to Show

"Those who ride seldom experience anything more gratifying than the thrill of winning their first blue ribbon."

— STEPHEN O. HAWKINS

O NCE YOUR INSTRUCTOR has decided that you have progressed to the point where you are ready to compete in a horse show, there is a lot to do to get prepared for the big day. Your instructor should select the appropriate show and the classes that will suit you best. Find out if you or your instructor should do the paperwork in advance or at the show. Be sure to bring a check to pay for your classes.

Horse Talk

equitation:
A class judged on the rider's seat, position, turnout, and control of the horse.

hunter:
A class judged on performance, manners, way of going, and style over a course of natural jumps.

jumper:
A class judged on time and faults over a set course of brightly painted jumps.

Preparations Before Horse Show Day

Check with your instructor to find out exactly where the show is, how to get there, and what time you should arrive. If you are riding a school horse, the stable will probably bring all the necessary tack and equipment. Even so, there is no harm in politely checking to see that everything you will need is packed.

Make sure your clothes are all clean and your boots are polished. Don't wait till the day before the show to check your clothes. Your parents won't appreciate doing ten errands at the last minute, so get everything together a few days ahead of time. This is not a bad habit to get into early in your riding career.

If you care for and transport the horse yourself, have everything in order and packed the night before, so there are no delays in the morning.

Attire

A young rider looks well turned out in jodhpurs and jodhpur boots or laced paddock boots. Buff or tan is the

Horses and ponies need a few sips of water if they are working hard and the weather is warm.

A second-place win! This rider has the correct jodhpur straps properly in place for competing in a horse show. The leather strap under her knee is buckled with the strap end facing toward the rear of the pony. The elastic strap clamps to her jodhpurs and goes on the outside of her boots. These straps keep the jodhpurs in place. Without them, the pants ride up and twist.

usual color for jodhpurs. When you are past the pony and limit **equitation** divisions and are showing in open equitation, **hunter** or **jumper** classes, it's time to wear breeches and boots. Ready-made stretch breeches usually fit well and last a long time if they are properly cared for. They should be washed in cold water and line dried or sent to the cleaners. A clothes dryer will ruin the strapping (leather patches) on the knees of your pants.

Boots will probably be your most expensive item of clothing. For the best appearance and fit, invest in a pair of black dress boots or laced field boots. Unlined boots will be softer (and therefore more comfortable), and will allow a better feel of the horse. A careful shopper may find some decent ready-made boots or secondhand boots that are comfortable and fit well. In recent years, readymades have improved markedly, so be sure to search them out before you succumb to the huge expense of custom-made boots.

Hair How-To

When a rider graduates from the pony ranks and beginner equitation, it's time for breeches and tall boots, and for girls to put up their hair under the hunt cap.

Girls should not wait until the horse show to put up their hair the first time. Practice at home until you have it down pat. If you want to look poised and polished at your first horse show and every one thereafter, tidy hair is a key factor. Keep in mind that your hat will fit correctly if you buy it to fit you with your hair up, but it will be way too loose if you settle for a ponytail when you ride at home. Boys should keep their hair short enough for a neat appearance.

Neatly braided pigtails (right) are cute for young girls (up to 10 or 12 years) still wearing jodhpurs. The matching ribbon in the pony's tail is a nice touch — okay for local shows but not for the big A shows.

1. Here Clementine covers her hair with a hairnet and pulls it down over her ears to a very low ponytail in the back. Then she fastens it securely with an elastic or a hair clip, tucking wispy hairs inside the hairnet.

2. Next she flips up the ends and holds them with one hand as she slips the hat on from back to front. Some riders like to secure the ends with a hair clip or bobby pins.

3. Once the hat is on and the chin snap securely fastened, she checks that all loose ends are tucked in.

With her neatly braided hair, well-fitting shirt and blazer, gloves, and helmet, Renick is properly turned out for show day.

Brianne is ready for a full day of horse showing. She has everything she needs in her backpack, including a warm jacket, crop, spurs, and healthy snacks for energy.

You will look your best in neat, unobtrusive riding clothes. Of course, nothing fits quite so well as custom-made shirts and jackets, but most riders can get nearly the same effect by having a ready-made coat altered to fit. A plain navy blue or dark green coat with dark buttons is a good choice. Avoid loud colors and bright plaids.

Girls' ratcatcher shirts or chokers should be in solid pastel colors or white. A choker or shirt collar must fit perfectly. Anything too large or baggy looks very sloppy indeed. A few well-placed stitches on a big collar and choker can make all the difference. Many girls put monograms on their chokers in colors that coordinate with their jackets. This is a nice touch. Wear the absolute minimum of jewelry. Boys should wear conservative ties that are neatly tacked down — not flapping in the wind.

Gloves are a matter of taste and personal preference. If you wear them, they should be dark brown. I think there is just as good a feel with gloves on as without them, and they give you a more polished look in equitation classes. In rainy weather they are essential, because the reins get very slippery.

Helmets and Hard Hats

As for headgear, a USEF-approved helmet is mandatory every time you ride your pony. A great deal of research has dramatically improved the protection helmets offer us. Your local tack shop can advise you which hat is the most protective. **Be sure the chin strap is tight.**

Spurs and Crops

Whether or not you wear spurs depends on your expertise as a rider, your horse's disposition, and the situation at hand. If you wear spurs before you have achieved good control of your seat, hands, and lower legs, there is a risk of getting into trouble, as an unintentional jab can turn the quietest pony into a runaway. Spurs are more often necessary in hot weather than in cold, and more often in small, spooky indoor rings than in open fields. Still, some horses are so sluggish that they need prodding, even in the biggest field on the coldest, windiest day. You must rely on your trainer's judgment, and use your own judgment as well, when deciding whether to wear spurs.

I prefer Prince of Wales spurs to the hammerhead type. To me, they look more graceful and elegant. They come in lengths from ½ inch to 1½ inches, so you can buy exactly the length that suits your needs. Most riders find eventually that they need a variety of spurs of different lengths to be able to deal with all situations.

I believe a crop is a necessary aid for every rider who is past the beginning stage. Almost any horse can learn to accept the crop, no matter how tense and nervous he may be, and by using it you can often prevent a serious situation from developing. Learn to carry the crop in either hand comfortably. In most cases, it should be used behind the saddle, but occasionally a tap on the shoulder is useful when a horse is about to pop out his shoulder on a turn. Crops come in a variety of lengths. A 14-inch crop is long enough to be effective but short enough to be held easily and out of the horse's range of vision.

Shaefer's mother attaches her number. She will need to tighten her chin strap before mounting.

Spur Styles

Prince of Wales

hammerhead

Informal shows, unrecognized by the USEF, often require only that riders have the proper helmet, boots, and jodhpurs. A riding jacket and riding shirt are not always necessary. Check to be sure, though.

This little girl is riding in her first show. Her cowboy boots and borrowed blue blazer are fine for this local event. Her pony is clean and braided.

Horse Show Checklist

HORSE

❑ Saddle
❑ Saddle pads (fleece or foam)
❑ Square quilted baby pad (to wear under saddle pad while schooling)
❑ Girth
❑ Martingale and/or breastplate
❑ Bridle(s)
❑ Extra bits if necessary

❑ Grooming box
❑ One or two pails
❑ Hay net/extra bale of hay
❑ Grain, if needed

❑ Blankets
❑ Sheet
❑ Rainsheet
❑ Coolers

RIDER

❑ Hat
❑ Hairnet, clips, and bobby pins for the girls
❑ Shirt and tie or choker
❑ Jodhpurs or breeches
❑ Boots (polished)
❑ Spurs
❑ Crop
❑ Gloves
(all clean and in good condition)

❑ Directions to the horse show
❑ A check for entry fees
❑ USEF height card (ponies)

Because weather can change, always bring:
❑ Raincoat
❑ Warm parka
❑ Rubbers

Show Day!

Finally the day of your first horse show arrives. Don't forget to allow plenty of time to get up, get dressed, and get to the show, and be sure you have directions, and money for the entry fees.

When you get to the show, check in with your teacher for information about entering your classes and warming up. You will probably ride around the grounds and work your horse on the flat and even over some fences. Some shows permit schooling in the ring. If the ring is crowded, do not let the other horses distract or rattle you. Just calmly tune in to your trainer, go on with your plan, and finish up when the call to clear the ring is heard.

Many riders "shoot themselves in the foot" by not being organized on show day and having to think about minor details, when they should be focusing on the competition itself.

At a large stable, experienced riders and grooms load the horses while the beginners watch and learn.

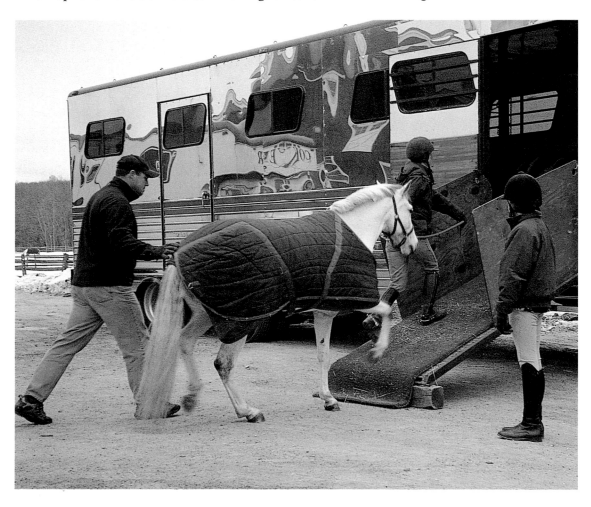

Lindsay trailers her pony from home to the show. Here she loads him into the trailer.

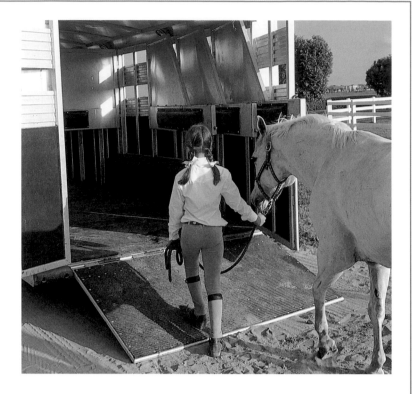

Then she ties him securely in the trailer.

After their trip, the ponies are unloaded.

Part of the fun of horse showing is competing with friends.

The mane and tail below have been braided by a professional and make the horse look sleek and tidy. Anyone who perseveres can learn to braid well, but practice at home before the show.

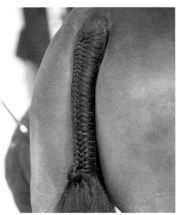

The Leadline class is popular at horse shows. Here, world-class rider Norman Dello Joio leads a young friend.

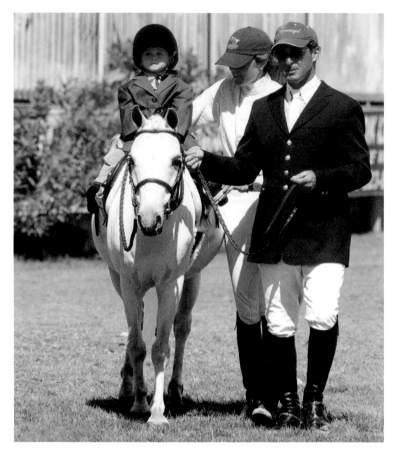

Divisions at Horse Shows

Let's talk about the divisions that are available at most local horse shows. Leadline and Walk-Trot are self-explanatory. In some Leadline classes riders are asked to trot, so in those classes you must know how to post. Walk-trot equitation riders are expected to know how to post, and also to be on the correct diagonal.

The Short Stirrup division is usually open to riders under 12 years (or sometimes under 10). Classes in this division are on the flat and over tiny jumps, and even cross rails are offered. Sometimes the horse is judged and sometimes the rider's equitation is judged. Read the details in the prize list so you know the judge's focus. If you get in the habit of doing this, it can save you a lot of grief later on.

The USEF recognizes a variety of horse shows: A shows are the most competitive, B and C less competitive, local shows and unrecognized shows are even more informal. Any division may be offered at any show. Therefore, lead-line and short stirrup classes can be held at A shows as shown in the picture above.

Once a rider has progressed beyond Short Stirrup, there are numerous Equitation classes, starting with Maiden on the Flat (walk, trot, and canter) and Over Fences of 2'. Maiden Equitation classes are for riders who have never won a blue-ribbon prize in a USEF-rated horse show; Novice, for riders who have not won three blue ribbons; Limit, six blues, and so on. Children's Hunter classes are for ponies and horses to be judged on their style of jumping over low jumps: 2' to 2' 9" for ponies, 3' for horses. Children's Equitation classes are open to all children, regardless of previous winnings. Often Children's Equitation classes are divided by fence height, usually ranging between 2' and 3'.

The Pony Hunter division offers three sections: Small, 12.2 hands and under; Medium, 13.2 hands and under; and Large, 14.2 hands and under. Horses and ponies are measured by *hands.* One hand equals 4 inches. Simple arithmetic tells us that Smalls may not exceed 50 inches; Mediums, 54 inches; and Larges, 58 inches.

Schaefer warms up her pony for their jumping class; she is sitting well, and the pony gives her a good jump.

A new and very exciting division is Pony Jumpers. For children who ride on a budget it is truly a boon because a fancy, expensive pony is not necessary. It can be a scruffy, ugly little creature; all that matters is whether or not it leaves up the jumps. This division has created thousands of jobs for genuinely useful ponies and favors aggressive riders who are not afraid to go fast and turn short to a jump to beat the clock. Soon we will see a whole new crop of graduates from this division pushing their junior peers — and eventually national and international show jumping stars as well.

Every pony and horse shown by a junior must be measured by two officials from the USEF at its first USEF-recognized horse show. The pony receives a temporary card at that point, stating its height, and later a current measurement card. Any pony's height may be questioned anytime, so riders must be sure to bring the card to every USEF-recognized horse show.

Brianne shows excellent form: nice following hand, deep heels, sitting in the middle of her horse — not ahead or behind — and eyes fixed on the next jump. Wonderful!

Annie is receiving some last-minute instruction in the warm-up area.

Certain ponies are more competitive than others, but on a given day anything can happen!

Good school ponies have been known to jump up and win a Pony Hunter class, especially the first class in a spooky ring. That's part of the fun of horse showing . . . you never know who will be the winner!

Ponies that show in the Pony Hunter division, especially at the "A" horse shows' competitive events, are usually fancier than those in the Children's Hunter Pony division. By "fancier," I mean prettier to look at, and their way of going and style of jumping are often superior. Some of the best teaching ponies are traditionally shown in the Children's Hunter Pony division. That division is perfect for low-intermediate riders.

The next step up from the Children's Hunter division and the Pony Hunter division are the Mini Medal and Mini Maclay classes, where the rider's seat and control are judged over a course of 3'3" jumps. Usually the courses are similar to and often exactly the same as the big Hunter Seat Equitation classes: the USEF Medal and the ASPCA Maclay. Riders compete in those classes at local USEF-recognized shows as well as at the A-, B- and C-rated events. The "big" equitation events — the PHA, the ASPCA Maclay, the USEF Medal, the USET and the Washington International Horse Show — are beyond the scope of this book.

Schaefer is waiting to enter the ring. She is beautifully turned out. Notice the heart on her choker, a nice touch instead of the traditional monogram. I wish her chin strap were tighter, however. Chatting with a friend, she is not tense and worried about her impending performance, but relaxed and enjoying it all, as she should be.

These two best friends enjoy their time together between classes at the show.

Classes on the Flat

The Hunter Seat Equitation judge will compare the basic position of the riders — seat, legs, and hands — as well as their control over the horses or ponies. He or she also will be judging the riders' influence on their mounts. The horses or ponies should be well balanced, straight on the long sides of the ring and nicely bent around the ends.

Show what you know about riding on the flat. Before the class starts, do a few transitions to catch the judge's eye. When the judge calls for the class to reverse, instead of just turning around, demonstrate a turn on the forehand. A horse show is just that. You should show off how good you are and hide your faults. For instance, if you bounce around at the sitting trot, trot your horse very slowly, so he doesn't bounce you much, and hide behind another horse if possible.

Inexperienced show riders usually rush to obey the judge's commands. Be as prompt as possible, but not at the cost of getting the wrong lead. When there is a call to canter, position your horse by squeezing him with your outside leg behind the girth. This prepares him to canter on the proper lead before you actually ask for the canter. In your zeal to be seen by the judge, however, make sure you are not rude to your fellow competitors. Try not to cut them off or, worse yet, bump into them!

The first trot is especially important, because that is when most judges pick the entries they want to use in the final lineup. If the judge misses you at the first trot, the most you can hope for is a low ribbon.

Before entering the ring, make sure you know if the flat class is an Equitation class or a Hunter Under Saddle class. In the former, the rider is judged; in the latter, the horse. Traditionally, in Equitation classes the rider shows her horse with a somewhat shorter rein than she would in an Under Saddle class.

In flat classes make sure the judge sees you. Check out where she is sitting or standing. Try to stay by yourself as much as possible, so she can really watch you ride. Sometimes, as an instructor, even I have difficulty finding my riders in the ring.

This young girl is demonstrating very good eye control. As she rounds the turn, she is looking where she is going, and her pony will follow her eye.

"Trot, Please!"

The procedure for flat classes is usually (but not always) as follows, so listen carefully in case the judge varies his commands. When all competitors have gathered in the ring, the command will be to walk. Find a place by yourself so the judge can see you on the first trot. After the trot the judge will probably call for a walk and then the canter. Then you will reverse and repeat that pattern.

When the judge has made her decision, you will be told to line up. Trot right in and line up in the center, so your number is right in front of her, in the hope that she will want to double-check your number and give you a ribbon: blue for first; red, second; yellow, third; white, fourth; pink, fifth; green, sixth; purple, seventh; or brown, eighth. Any ribbon is a good ribbon.

Hunter Under Saddle

Hunter Under Saddle classes are also judged on the flat, but in these classes the horse or pony is being judged. "Light contact with the horse's or pony's mouth is required," according to the USEF rule book. Manners and way of moving are compared.

Final instructions. Here the instructor, Peter Lutz, is explaining exactly how to ride a certain part of the course. The rider is obviously paying close attention, as she should.

The horse or pony should be quiet and obedient, but not dull. He should prick his ears and seem happy and alert. A sour expression and ears pinned back will be penalized. He should be well balanced and move close to the ground with a long, slow, sweeping stride at the trot and at the canter. If he has a good trot and canters with a high stride, show off at the trot and hide at the canter, and vice versa. Show his good points and hide his faults.

Classes Over Fences

For the classes over fences, be sure that you know the course and try to watch as much as possible before you mount. Review the course plan with your teacher and walk the course if that is permitted. The jumping order and a diagram of the course will be posted at the in-gate. As you study the course, make sure that if there is a dotted line, you know where it is. A dotted line across the ring on the diagram means that anyone who crosses that line while making his circle will automatically be eliminated. Dotted lines are great time-savers and must be observed even in Short Stirrup classes.

Allow five to ten horses in front of you in planning the warm-up time. For the first class you may need the extra time of ten horses. After that, five should be

Walking the course. Here the riders are inspecting the course, pacing off the distances between the jumps, not forgetting to notice problems in the terrain — footing too deep or too hard, as well as uphill and downhill grades — and generally getting a feel of the ring.

In a Children's Jumper class, Nicholas Dello Joio is looking for the next jump in a timed jump-off. Fast jump-offs are a family tradition; his father is world class show jumper, Norman Dello Joio.

enough because you will not need to do as much. You do not want to be ready too early and stand around a long time before you go in. Being rushed at the last minute is hectic and equally inappropriate. It's important to develop a sense of time, so you give yourself enough but not too much.

You should also take into consideration your mount's temperament. Placid horses do better if they go right in the ring after schooling. High-strung and nervous ones need a few minutes to settle after schooling before they compete. If you do have to wait around on a placid horse, smack him with your stick or give him a good kick before you enter the ring. (Make sure he is awake!) However, if you are rushed at the last minute with a high-strung horse, go directly to the in-gate when called. Once in the ring, walk a few steps and soothe him with your voice before picking up the canter and starting your round.

As Annie waits to enter the ring, her instructor, Mary Manfredi, reviews the course with her.

Riding the Course

Whether the class is a Short Stirrup Crossrail class or the Olympic Games, once in the ring, rider and mount must concentrate on the job at hand. Some riders are less easily distracted and therefore more able than others to remember their plan. To some extent, concentration is a learned skill and one that riders need to develop from the very beginning. Reviewing the course several times in your mind before going into the ring will help you concentrate while you are actually in the ring.

The opening circle establishes the pace for the course. A sluggish horse needs to get above his pace early in the circle and then settle into it, so he is not behind the eight ball at the first fence. An eager horse, however, will build as he goes around the course, so the rider must be sure to slow him down on the ends of the ring or he will be ahead of himself and going much too fast by the end of the course.

A general rule of thumb: Be ready to override the difficult parts and be careful not to override the simpler parts.

Remember, the good rider must be "tuned in" to his or her horse or pony. While analyzing the course, scope it out from your mount's point of view. Some show rings are impressive and some are spooky, just as some horses are easily impressed and some are easily frightened. "Know your horse as you analyze the course" should be the motto of any serious rider. Beyond the general look of the ring, figure out which lines, angles, and turns might post problems as well as which jumps look impressive or spooky.

Riders just starting their show careers should remember that at first they will need to rely on mounts that "show them where the jumps are" — old troopers who know their way around the ring. Young green horses are inappropriate for young green riders. Likewise, the difficult horse will never teach you to ride or make you a winner. Instead, he will have you soon searching around for another sport.

> "A real horseman not only knows why a horse reacts as he does, but usually anticipates his reactions."
>
> — C. W. Anderson

Brianne is on course, focused ahead, and looking good!

Schaefer is warming up her pony on the flat. The pony is nicely bent around her inside leg. The arc of his body corresponds to the arc of the circle. Schaefer's position is correct: heels down, a straight line from her elbow to the pony's mouth, and, most important, she is looking in to make the turn smoothly.

If you do not win a lot in the beginning, don't give up. Keep honing your skills and eventually you may be able to graduate to a fancier mount. The most important attribute for a rider to have is perseverance. The willingness to keep trying is a quality to be more valued than talent, the right build, wealth, or anything else. Learning to ride is not easy, and winning in competition does not usually happen right away.

Remember, when you ride into the ring, you are in a horse show. *Your job is to show you are the best.* The ring is yours for the next minute or two, so make the most of it! For some, showmanship comes naturally. Others have to work to develop it. Believe me, it is well worth developing.

Hunter Classes: Patterns

Pony Hunter and Children's Hunter courses are usually quite simple and straightforward. Generally, there are eight jumps: side, diagonal, side, diagonal, or a variation of that. Hunters are judged on "performance, manners, way of going, and style of jumping," according to USEF specifications. Performance is the horse's evenness and smoothness as he proceeds around the course: over the fences, between the fences, and around the turns. A hunter should snatch his knees up and round his back, because when the performances of several horses are about the same, the style of jumping will determine who will be the winner. As in the Under Saddle classes, "the way of going" is also either a plus or a minus.

When I am judging, the manners of a child's mount are particularly important. Another important factor is suitability for the rider. Size as well as temperament should be considered. The only picture worse than a huge child on a tiny pony is a tiny child overmounted on a huge horse.

The jog. In the rated Hunter divisions, the ponies or horses must jog for soundness in the order of the judge's preference. The rider removes the saddle and martingale, brings the reins over the horse's head, and leads him trotting into the ring in the order in which she was called. These riders are awaiting the judge's results.

Equitation Classes

In Equitation classes the rider is being judged, but of course the overall picture can make the difference. A horse and rider combination that seems to fit together will excel over the odd-looking pair if the performances (that is, their executions of the course) are equivalent.

From the opening circle, the rider's basic position and control are being judged as well as the actual execution of the course. Accuracy is of utmost importance. The rider must "nail" the eight or however many jumps there are. Particularly at the lower levels of Hunter Seat Equitation (Maiden, Novice, and even Limit classes), the rider's position is carefully scrutinized, for in the early stages most riders have not developed a style of their own. At that level — and really at all levels — the basics are what count. If you have applied what you have learned in your lessons and in this book, you should be able to demonstrate sound basics in the show ring.

Here the trainer has thrown a blanket over the jump to give it a different, scary look. Plain rails in the schooling area are different from the colored walls and gates in the ring, so it is helpful to jump something "scary" outside to know how much leg you will need in the ring. Shaefer's pony, leaving the ground reluctantly, needs a "punch off the ground" to make sure he jumps the fence with enthusiasm.

After the Class

When you have finished your round, whether it was good, bad, or mediocre, analyze your performance. Review the entire course slowly and carefully in your mind, figuring out which parts were good and which were not so good. Then try to figure out why. Probably your round was not perfect; probably it was not totally horrible either. Be realistic and objective as you sort out your thoughts (much easier said than done!). This is a skill we all must learn to develop. If you have a trainer or ground person helping you, review your performance with him or her as well. You will find over the years that plain old common sense is your best tool as you review your courses.

A young rider who keeps her horse at home and comes to my barn for the occasional lesson complained to me one day that her horse was stopping all the time at the shows. (At home and during her lessons, we had the opposite problem; he hurried to the jumps. To correct his rushing, she often circled in front of the jumps until he settled.)

Resistances come in pairs. If you kick your pony forward, be prepared to slow him if he overreacts and goes to fast.

Common sense helped us find the solution. Obviously, the horse found the unfamiliar ring impressive and the jumps scary. He needed to be "ridden up to the jump." In other words, the young rider had to kick him to get him up to the jumps, a new experience for her as well.

At the next show she rode up to the jumps and he never even thought of stopping. At that show the rider learned firsthand that a horse's resistance comes in pairs. When she kicked him to the jumps, he would bolt away upon landing. She had to be ready for the second resistance and slow him down immediately upon landing.

You will find that horse shows will help you discover your own and your mount's weaknesses and strengths. The thinking rider will be able to turn those weaknesses into strengths. No matter how bad a show you have, you will always gain something from it. Sometimes things have to get worse before they get better. Make yourself think positively, even if you do not have a good day.

At the end of the day remember your teammate. I bet Lindsay has a carrot in her hand for her pony.

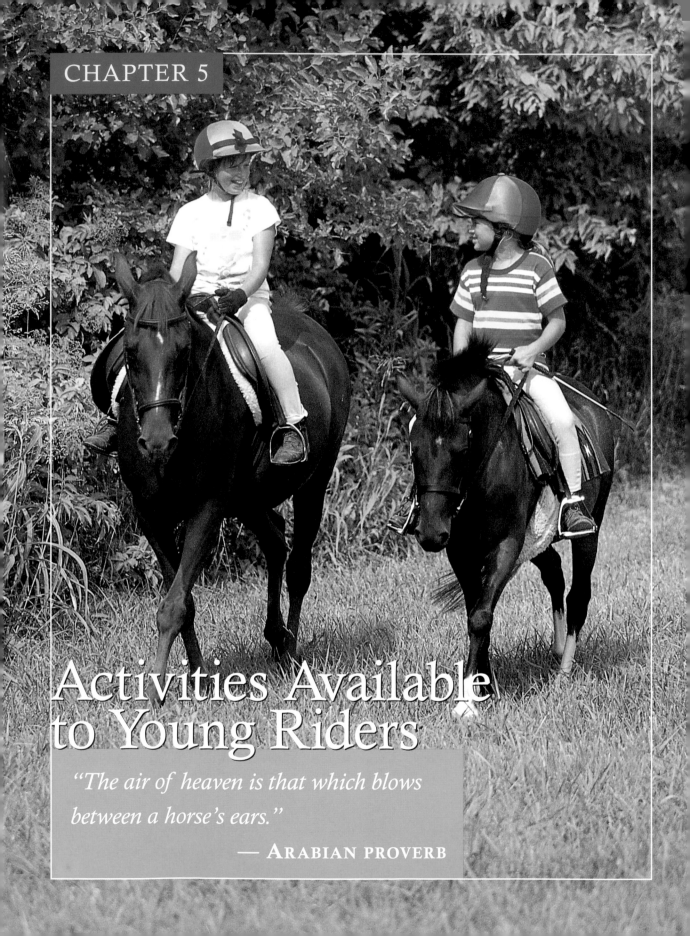

CHAPTER 5

Activities Available to Young Riders

"The air of heaven is that which blows between a horse's ears."

— **ARABIAN PROVERB**

T HERE IS AN OLD SAYING, "There are many roads to Rome," and so it is with riding horses. The Olympics and World Championships can look very far away to a pony rider watching riders and horses jump huge fences in the various Grand Prix. Persistence is probably the most important trait for a serious rider to have. As Denny Emerson, the Olympic Three-Day Event rider, so aptly said, "You have to stick with it."

Horse Talk

dressage:
A combination of precise movements on the flat that display a high level of training on the part of both horse and rider.

gymkhana:
A program of competitive mounted games, usually with a timed element. Events may be for individuals or teams.

Enjoying Your Horse

In riding there are good days, but there are also a lot of bad days. A thousand things can happen: a lame or sick horse, a judge doesn't like you, you miss all the distances. You have to be tough to take all that can go wrong, but the good days are thrilling. If the pressure of competing does not appeal to you, there are many other ways to enjoy riding horses: trail rides, fox hunts, and hunter paces, to name a few.

Horses can be enjoyed in many ways at many levels at all stages of our lives. Young aggressive riders enjoy competition, but in later years riding for pleasure is truly a pleasure. While competing riders should ride often under super-vision to hone their skills, pleasure riders will find to their delight that riding a horse is a little like riding a bike. For instance, once you know how to post, you never forget. Having been in the business for almost 40 years, I am delighted when some of my former students come back as mothers and fathers eager for their own children to ride. And often

If you are interested in competing, the USEF is a good source of information about all disciplines. I urge all serious young riders to become members. See page 121, for contact information.

Polo clinics, camps, and children's leagues can be found in many areas of the country. Polo uses a variety of skills and is a great way to have fun on horseback.

while the kids are here for lessons, the parents will exercise a horse for me or just go for a ride in the woods.

For the competitive rider, there are horse shows — hunters, jumpers, equitation, the various breed divisions. Competition is also keen in the **dressage** arena and in three-phase events where dressage, cross country, and stadium jumping comprise a complete test of horse and rider: precision, endurance, and versatility. Endurance rides test just that and for variety there are rodeos, **gymkhanas**, polo, vaulting, hunter paces, horse racing, steeplechasing, and point-to-point, to name just a few activities available to young riders who have learned the basics of equitation. For those seeking action, fox hunting is an exciting sport. Animal lovers and nature lovers of all ages can enjoy leisurely trail rides and/or galloping through the countryside once they demonstrate reasonable competence in the ring and presuming they are mounted on reliable safe horses.

The very young, the timid, the aged, and the infirm should ride in well-supervised enclosed areas. Of course, there are countless exceptions to these guidelines. The most outstanding one was a Frenchman I knew as a child who fox-hunted until well into his 90s.

The rest of us need to be safety conscious and unembarrassed to rely on the expertise of professionals in the field. Horses are big strong animals, but if properly handled, they are not at all dangerous. Indeed, they can be our best friends. The charisma of the horse is proved

This boy is participating in a hunter pace event. Cross-country riding develops a rider's courage and skills.

every day in such unlikely places as New York City, where people often stop to stroke the patient carriage horses that stand outside the Plaza Hotel, always ready to give us a ride through Central Park — not the worst substitute for a peaceful ride through the woods.

This mom is sharing her love of horses with her two daughters. Most people, whether they live in apartments in the city or roam free in the country, love horses in their own way. Some ride for fun, some ride for medals, some are happy just to pet their soft noses and look into their dark lovely eyes.

Learning More

If you are interested in competing, the United States Equestrian Federation offers a wealth of information about all disciplines. I urge every serious young rider to become a member. A second good source of information is *The Chronicle of the Horse,* a weekly magazine published in Middleburg, Virginia. *The Chronicle* prints summaries of all major events here and abroad, as well as articles of general interest. *The Chronicle* is an official publication and offers links on its Web site to many organizations: Masters of Foxhounds Association of America; United States Equestrian Team, Inc.; The United States Pony

Gymkhanas are a fun way to enjoy your horse and test your riding skills.

Clubs, Inc.; The National Riding Commission of the American Alliance of Health, Physical Education, Recreation and Dance; Foxhound Club of North America; Roster of Packs of the National Beagle Club of America, Inc.; United States Dressage Federation, Inc.; American Vaulting Association; North American Riding for the Handicapped Association, Inc.; and Intercollegiate Horse Show Association.

This girl from Ireland has a determined look on her face that tells me she'll have that pony marching around the ring, down the road, and through the woods. She is wearing a junior model of the back protection mandatory from pony club to international competition.The pony is wearing rope side reins to prevent him from tasting the sweet green grass as they travel through the fields.

The two national organizations whose local chapters offer the best programs for young riders are Pony Club and the 4-H Club of America. which you may reach through the Cooperative Extension 4-H Agent of any county in the United States. Contact them directly for information about the chapters in your area (see page 121). Some of the best riders in the nation have come up through the ranks of Pony Club and 4-H.

For those who simply want to ride for pleasure, I say, "Just do it." In our high-powered, pressure-filled world, there is no better relaxation, no greater pleasure, than a ride on a nice horse on a beautiful day, and if the scenery is lovely, so much the better. Even an ordinary ride on an ordinary horse on an ordinary day is a lot of fun. The old saying is true: "The outside of a horse is good for the inside of a man" — or woman — no matter how young or old.

This young 4-H rider has a new horse and she can't wait to get started with lessons. There is no telling what they will accomplish together!

For those who have no real horses to ride, there are lots of imaginary ones. Haley and Lindsay have theirs jumping beautifully, getting them prepared for the next show.

4-H The youth education branch of the Cooperative Extension Service, part of the United States Department of Agriculture. Each state and county have an office that oversees programs, including equestrian. Canada has a similar 4-H program. See page 121 for contact information.

Action The degree of flexion of the joints of the legs during movement; also reflected in head, neck, and tail carriage. High, snappy action is desirable in some classes, while easy, ground-covering action is the goal in other classes.

Aid An aid is a signal from the rider to the horse that causes the horse to react in a particular way. An aid is almost never used alone, but rather in conjunction with other aids. The rider's natural aids are the voice, hands, seat, weight, legs, and upper body. Artificial aids include whips, and spurs.

ASTM/SEI (American Standard for Testing Materials and Safety Equipment Institute) Riding helmets with an ASTM/SEI label meet or exceed all ASTM safety standards.

Beat A single step in a gait, involving one leg or two. For example, the walk is a four-beat gait, with each beat marked by a single leg, one at a time, 1-2-3-4. The trot is a two-beat gait, stepped off by two legs landing at the same time. The canter is a three-beat gait.

Behind the girth One of the two fundamental leg positions for a rider. Positioning one's legs at the girth means placing them directly over the horse's center of balance. Positioning legs behind the girth means moving them back 2 to 4 inches from the center, allowing control of the hindquarters.

Bending the horse A series of actions taken by a rider that cause a horse to flex its neck and body, most often during turns, but also in higher-level movements. Bending the horse is often necessary to maintain the balance of horse and rider and to prevent falls.

Breeches Riding pants that come in a variety of styles, but generally are tight on the calf so they can be worn with tall boots. They usually have reinforced patches on the inner leg to help the rider maintain a safe position, protect the knees from bruising, and enhance the durability of the breeches. *See also* Chaps, Jodhpurs.

Broke A broke horse is a trained animal that accepts being handled and ridden.

Canter The English term for a three-beat gait with right and left leads. A very fast canter is called a gallop.

Cavelletti A series of parallel poles or rails that are placed on the ground or on low supports, spaced at a distance roughly equivalent to a horse's trotting or cantering stride. Instructors use them to prepare students for higher-level riding. The cavelletti is also an exercise in agility for the horse. See Ground poles.

Cavesson The noseband of a bridle. A longeing cavesson is a reinforced noseband with rings for attaching longeing reins.

Chaps Leather or suede leggings that protect the rider's pants and legs. Originally designed for cowboys riding through heavy brush and still a standard item of Western riding apparel, chaps are often used by English riders as well. Half chaps zip over the lower leg. *See* Breeches, Jodhpurs.

Chipping in What a horse does when he finds himself too close to a jump to make the leap in his natural stride. He will break stride and jump in a steep vertical arc, often failing to clear the bar. This is also known as popping.

Choker The collar of a type of shirt (called a ratcatcher) worn by women during hunter/jumper and low-level dressage competitions. *See* Ratcatcher, Stock tie.

Class The various kinds of riding and show events defined by a set of criteria. Some classes judge the quality or conformation of the horse, others are concerned with the horse's performance, and still others evaluate the skills of the rider. Classes can also be determined by the age and breed of the horse or by the age and gender of the rider.

Collection A state of organized movement and balance that characterizes a well-trained horse. A collected horse is agile, light on his feet, and responsive. *See* Engagement.

Combined training/eventing A competition designed to test training and riding skills in the areas of dressage, cross-country riding, and stadium jumping.

Contact The pressure applied to the horse's mouth through the reins. *See* Aid.

Crest The top of the horse's neck along the mane.

Crest release A maneuver in which the rider rests her hands on the horse's crest while the horse is jumping in order to maintain balance.

Crop A short riding stick or whip used to reinforce leg aids while in the saddle.

Cross-canter Cantering with the front legs on a lead different from the hind. Also called disunited, this is not a comfortable gait to ride and is generally undesirable.

Cross rail A small jump consisting of two poles in an x shape, used to teach young horses and riders to jump the center of the jump.

Cross-tie A means of tying a horse by attaching ropes or chains from each side of an aisle to the side rings of the halter.

Diagonal A pair of legs moving together at the trot (right front and left hind or left front and right hind). When posting, the rider sits as the inside hind leg hits the ground and rises as the inside front leg lifts off. Remember to "rise and fall with the (front) leg on the wall!"

Direct rein A method of using the rein in which the rider communicates directly with the horse by putting pressure on his mouth. For example, a turn to the right is accomplished by increasing pressure on the right rein so the horse responds by giving into the pressure. *See* Aid, Direct rein, Indirect rein, Leading rein.

Disunited Cantering in different leads front and hind. Also called cross-cantering.

Dressage A combination of precise movements on the flat that display a

high level of training on the part of both the horse and the rider.

Engagement A condition in which a moving horse has shifted his weight to the hindquarters and is striding forward with the hind legs. Being engaged increases the horse's energy and propulsion (forward movement). An engaged horse has a rounded top line, lowered croup, and flexed abdominal muscles. *See* Collection.

Equitation The art of riding. In equitation classes, the rider is judged on correctness of form, proper use of the aids, and control over the horse. The main equitation classes are hunt seat equitation, Western horsemanship (or stock seat equitation), and saddle seat equitation.

Eventing *See* Combined training/eventing.

Finished horse A horse that is properly trained for a particular purpose. *See* Green.

Flying lead change When a horse changes from one lead to another while cantering without breaking stride. A simple lead change involves coming back to a trot or walk to pick up the opposite lead.

Forehand The horse's head, neck, shoulders, and front legs.

Forward seat A style of hunt seat riding in which the rider uses a slightly shorter stirrup and balances her weight somewhat ahead of the vertical for all work above a walk. This position allows a rider to stay balanced over larger jumps. *See* Aid, Deep seat, Forward seat, Seat.

Gait A specific pattern of foot movements such as the walk, trot, and canter. Most horses naturally use these three gaits, but some breeds are known for a fourth gait, which may be a smooth, running walk, a very exaggerated, high-stepping trot, or a four-bear gait called the slow gait and, when faster, the rack.

Green Used to describe both horses and riders who are relatively inexperienced. A good rule of thumb is that green riders need experienced horses and vice versa. *See* Finished horse.

Ground poles Poles placed just in front of the vertical elements of a jump in order to help the horse judge the takeoff point. *See* Cavalletti.

Ground training When a horse is worked by a handler on the ground instead of by a rider in the saddle. Ground training, or in-hand work, is very important, and includes barn manners, longeing, and ground driving.

Gymkhana A program of competitive mounted games, usually with a timed element. Events may be for individuals or teams.

Half-halt A signal to help the horse maintain balance during changes of gait, direction, or speed or maintain consistent speed. The rider essentially calls the horse to attention by increasing contact with the lower legs while simultaneously increasing pressure on the reins ever so slightly and releasing. *See* Aid.

Half seat In English riding this term can mean one of two things: either pushing more weight into the heel and inclining the body slightly forward or rising slightly in the stirrups while at the canter or hand gallop to allow the horse more freedom of movement. *See* Two-point seat.

Hand Horses are measured from the highest point of the withers to the ground in units called hands. One hand equals 4 inches. 14.2 means (14 hands x 4 inches) + 2 inches, which is 56 inches + 2 inches = 58 inches.

Helmet All riders should wear helmets every time they get on a horse. Be sure the helmet is designed specifically for horseback riding and meets the standards set by ASTM/SEI. *See* ASTM/SEI.

Horsemanship Exhibition of a rider's skill, while riding his horse.

Hunter class A class that is sometimes part of a hunter-jumper show and sometimes held separately. Hunter classes are judged on performance, manners, way of going, and style of jumping.

Indirect rein Laying the rein against the horse's neck as a signal to encourage the horse to bend in a certain direction. *See* Aid, Direct rein, Indirect rein, Leading rein.

Inside (leg or rein) The leg or rein to the inside of the space one is working in, whether an arena, paddock, or contained field. The inside leg or rein is the one seen by a person standing in the center of that space. In the open, the inside leg or rein is the one you desire the horse to bend around or move away from. *See* Outside.

Jodhpurs Pants worn in English riding that are designed to go over short boots. Jodhpurs (named for the area in India where they originated) are usually worn by young riders.

Jog Refers to the in-hand test for soundness in rated hunter classes.

Jumper class A class that is sometimes part of a hunter-jumper show and sometimes held separately. Jumper classes are judged on time and faults, with the fastest clean round winning. *See* Hunter class.

Junior A rider under eighteen years of age as of December 1.

Lead A specific footfall pattern at the canter in which the legs on the inside of the circle reach farther forward than the outside legs.

Leading rein A rein that tells the horse which way to go by gently moving his head in the correct direction. The rider applies a leading rein by moving her hand laterally away from the horse's neck in the direction she wants him to turn; the rein should not be pulled upward or downward. *See* Aid, Direct rein, Indirect rein.

Lead-line class Class in which a parent, instructor, or older friend leads a pony or horse while the young rider follows the judge's directions.

Leg up Getting a leg up is a way of mounting your horse with the assistance of another person rather than a mounting block. The rider faces the saddle with the reins gathered and bends her left leg at a 90-degree angle. The helper places both hands on the rider's lower leg and at the count of three, the rider jumps up off her right foot while the helper boosts her into the saddle.

Longe To work a horse at various gaits in a circle around you, usually on a 30-foot line. A long whip should be used to help cue the horse. Longeing is used to train young horses, to work off excess energy of a frisky horse before riding, and as a way for riders to focus on their seat without having to think about the reins.

Manners The attitude and habits of a horse. Ground manners refer to the horse's behavior while being handled from the ground instead of in the saddle.

Mouth, hard or soft A term describing the horse's responsiveness to the reins. A horse is said to have a soft mouth if he responds readily to cues from the reins. A hard-mouthed horse will resist cues and fight the bit. A hard mouth usually results from poor handling, by either a brutal rider or a series of inexperienced ones.

Near side The horse's left side.

Novice In general, an inexperienced, or green, rider. USEF denotes a novice as one who has not won three blue ribbons in a USEF recognized show.

Off side The horse's right side.

On the bit A horse is said to be "on the bit" when he is moving forward freely, yet yielding to the pressure of the bit. The rider's legs and back press the horse forward, while her hands keep a sensitive contact with his mouth. *See* Aid, Collection, Engagement.

On the forehand A horse moving on the forehand has too much weight on his front legs and is unbalanced. Because the hindquarters provide the primary propulsion, a horse needs to distribute his weight evenly to be engaged and moving well. *See* Collection, Engagement, On the bit.

Outside (leg or rein) The leg or rein on the outer edge of the space one is working in, whether an arena, paddock, or contained field. The outside leg or rein is the one not seen by a person standing in the center of that space. *See* Inside.

Overmounted Riding a horse that is too strong or temperamental for you.

Oxer An oxer is a spread jump with a front (the take-off side of the obstacle) and a back (landing side) element that are constructed either to be equal in height or with the front element slightly lower than the back. Normally only a single pole is used for the back element.

Pattern A prescribed order of maneuvers in a particular class such as equitation. Patterns, which include figure-eights, serpentines, and circles, are an important part of training for both horse and rider. *See* School figures.

Pony A horse that stands 58 inches (14.2 hands) or less. Pony classes are often divided into Small (under 12.2), Medium (under 13.2), and Large (under 14.2).

Pony Club There are hundreds of pony clubs in the United States designed to introduce young riders to the basics of horse care and English riding. See page 121 for contact information.

Popping *See* Chipping in.

Posting A way of riding to the English trot by rising and falling in the saddle with the horse's movement. *See* Diagonal.

Pulley rein A strong measure to be used only when a horse is running and out of control. The rider shortens the reins, plants one hand on the horse's neck, and pulls hard up and back on the other rein to bring the horse in a circle and to a halt.

Ratcatcher A collarless shirt worn with formal hunt or show attire. To complete the look, the rider wears either a bow tie of the same fabric as the shirt, a choker collar, or a stock tie, which wraps around the throat. *See* Choker, Stock tie.

Ring sour A negative attitude in a horse that does not enjoy working in an arena and looks for ways to leave the ring or quit working. Being ring sour is often a sign of boredom or overwork. He pins his ears and balks to show his distaste.

School figures Standard maneuvers that all beginning riders should master: circles, figure-eights, changes of direction, crossing the diagonal, and others. These figures provide an opportunity for the student to develop coordination of aids at various gaits. *See* Patterns.

Schooling show A show designed as practice for both novice and advanced riders. Often these shows have no affiliation with any equine organization, but they are a good way to gain experience for both rider and horse.

Seat The position in which the rider sits on the horse. There are a variety of seats that correspond to different disciplines. Along with the other aids, the seat is an important communication tool for the rider. *See* Aid.

Simple lead change To change the lead of the canter from one side to the other by slowing to a trot or walk or halting before picking up the opposite lead. *See* Flying lead change.

Stock tie A narrow white scarf worn with formal hunt or show attire. *See* Choker, Ratcatcher.

Stride The distance traveled in a particular gait, measured from the spot where one hoof hits the ground to where it next lands. Ten to 12 feet is the normal length of stride at the canter, for example.

Transition A change from one gait to another. An upward transition is to a faster gait; a downward one is to a slower one. Transitions should be made smoothly, with subtle aids from the rider and prompt responses from the horse.

Trot A two-beat diagonal gait in which the opposite pairs of legs move together (e.g., left front and right hind).

Turn on the forehand A turn in which the horse moves his hindquarters around his forequarters; his front feet remain virtually motionless while his hind feet step in a semicircle (180 degrees) so that he is facing the opposite direction.

Two-point seat or half-seat In a two-point seat, the rider stands slightly in the stirrups with her weight balanced and light contact on the reins. Her third point of contact, her seat, does not touch the saddle. This position allows the rider to absorb the motion of the trot or canter without bouncing on the horse's back.

USCTA The United States Combined Training Association oversees all horse trials for U.S. Equestrian Team tryouts, as well as for competition at lower levels.

USDF The United States Dressage Foundation has dozens of chapters around the country and provides information on dressage competition.

USEF The United States Equestrian Federation (formerly AHSA, American Horse Shows Association) is the national board that oversees all equine competition in the United States. The USEF regulates shows, works with the United States Equestrian Team to select team members, and trains officials for competitions. See page 121 for contact information.

USET The United States Equestrian Team oversees the selection and training of teams in six disciplines: Combined Driving, Dressage, Endurance Riding, Eventing (combined training), Reining, and Show Jumping.

Vertical A vertical jump involves height without width. It has one pair of standards (supports) and a single element that can consist of poles, gates, planks, or walls, alone or in combination.

Voice aid The voice is an important aid in handling and riding horses, in both giving specific instructions (many horses understand what "whoa" means, for example) and sending signals (a soothing tone can ease a nervous horse). *See* Aid.

Walk A four-beat, flat-footed gait.

Walk-trot classes Competition in which the only gaits called for are the walk and the trot. These classes are good experience for beginning riders.

Way of going The overall look of a horse as he moves, including his manners, natural impulsion, presence, and how he travels; in hunters, low to the ground is preferred.

Xenophon A fourth-century Greek soldier, Xenophon was an avid horseman whose book *On Horsemanship* contains many principles that are still standard practice. Horseback riding, he claimed, "makes the body healthy, improves the sight and hearing, and keeps men from growing old."

Contact Information

4-H Club
Find your local chapter through the Cooperative Extension 4-H agent of any county in the United States. Your telephone book will have the number.

Canadian 4-H Council
Carling Avenue, Building {#}26
Ottawa, Ontario K1A 0C6
www.4-h-canada.ca

Canadian Pony Club
Box 1127
Baldur, Manitoba R0K 0B0
www.canadianponyclub.org

USEF
United States Equestrian Federation (formerly USA Equestrian and American Horse Shows Association)
4047 Iron Works Parkway
Lexington, KY 40511-8483
www.equestrian.org

United States Pony Clubs, Inc.
4041 Iron Works Parkway
Lexington, KY 40511-8462
www.ponyclub.org

Page numbers in **boldface** indicate a chart.

Page numbers in *italics* indicate a photograph or illustration.

RECOMMENDED READING

Dutson, Judith. *Getting Your First Horse* (Storey Publishing, 1998)

Haas, Jessie. *Safe Horse, Safe Rider: A Young Rider's Guide to Responsible Horsekeeping* (Storcy Publishing, 1994)

Harris, Susan. *Grooming to Win: How to Groom, Trim, Braid and Prepare Your Horse for Show* (Howell Book House, 1991)

Harris, Susan. *The United States Pony Club Manual of Horsemanship* (Howell Book House, 1994)

Hill, Cherry. *101 Arena Exercises: A Ringside Guide for Horse & Rider* (Storey Publishing, 1995)

Hill, Cherry. *Becoming an Effective Rider: Developing Your Mind and Body for Balance and Unity* (Storey Publishing, 1991)

Hill, Cherry. *From the Center of the Ring* (Storey Publishing, 1988)

Hill, Cherry. *Horse Handling and Grooming: A Step-by-Step Photographic Guide to Mastering Over 100 Horsekeeping Skills* (Storey Publishing, 1997)

Hill, Cherry. *Horse Health Care: A Step-by-Step Photographic Guide to Mastering Over 100 Horsekeeping Skills* (Storey Publishing, 1997)

Hill, Cherry. *Stablekeeping: A Visual Guide to Safe and Healthy Horsekeeping* (Storey Publishing, 2000)

Hill, Cherry. *Trailering Your Horse: A Visual Guide to Safe Training and Traveling* (Storey Publishing, 2000)

Morris, George, H. *Hunter Seat Equitation* (Doubleday, 1990)

Smith, Mike. *Getting the Most from Riding Lessons* (Storey Publishing, 1998)

Steinkraus, William. *Reflections on Riding and Jumping: Winning Techniques for Serious Riders* (Trafalger Square, 1997)

Steinkraus, William. *Riding and Jumping* (Doubleday, 1969)